"It's A Fact"

"It's A Fact"

Harold "Dusty" Miller

A series of drawings originally published
in the "Isle of Man Examiner" during 1936-39.

THE MANX EXPERIENCE

Published by
The Manx Experience
24 Sunnybank Avenue : Birch Hill : Onchan : Isle of Man : IM3 3BW
on behalf of the family of the late Harold "Dusty" Miller

*The book has been enhanced by linking some of the drawings
to articles contained in the publications:
"Here is the News" and "Chronicles of the 20th Century" -
both of which relate Manx history in the form of radio reports,
and information found in "An Illustrated Encyclopedia of the Isle of Man".*

The Author and her family are indebted to Isle of Man Newspapers
for their unqualified agreement to the publication of this book.

*Printed in the Isle of Man by Mannin Media Group Limited
Media House : Cronkbourne : Douglas : Isle of Man : IM4 4SB : British Isles*

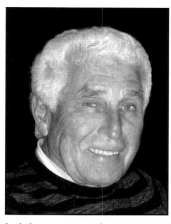

FOREWORD
by
Terry Cringle

The first time I encountered Dusty he was a scoutmaster and I was a Scout. It happened during the wartime 1940's when I was in camp at Glen Wyllin with the 8th Douglas. On the first morning, with a brisk wind blowing off the sea, he marshalled us on the shore for a swim. The sea was cold and we were reluctant. But Dusty led the way into the waves and we followed. There was something about him that made us do it. In January 1948 I left Douglas High School and joined the *Isle of Man Examiner* as a trainee reporter. I think by then Dusty had gone to the *Isle of Man Times* but everybody at the *Examiner* knew him and talked about him so I got to know him at second hand. Mind you, I might have got to know him better on a personal level. In my early teens I was deeply in love, at a distance, with his daughter Lesley. But she married somebody else. It's my recollection that Dusty's principal job with the newspapers was in advertising. His work as a cartoonist appears to have been a sideline. But it was a sideline which sold newspapers. This wasn't only because of *"It's a Fact"*. Dusty's political cartoons, both in and out of the time of the Second World War, were hugely entertaining and straight to the point, as were his caricatures of leading Island personalities, especially at social events, where his sharp sense of humour shone through. I might have come to know Dusty better with time but, just over a year after joining the *Examiner*, I was called up for two years National Service, returned to the *Examiner* briefly, and then left to work in newspapers in England throughout the 1950's. In 1962 I returned to the *Examiner*. But by then Dusty's time was running out. I had, however, developed a deep admiration for his draughtsmanship, especially in *"It's a Fact"*. People say the facts were not all as reliable as they might have been. But that doesn't matter. It was visual entertainment of a high order based on Manx history. And as any journalist will tell you, you can't get it right every time. I now have in frames on my walls a few original *"It's a Fact"* drawings because I like them so much. I would like to have more. But today the originals are almost impossible to find. Hardly any have survived. It seems that, once the drawings had been processed for publication by the engravers they were simply screwed up and thrown away. Yes, it is difficult to believe. But it is true. It's a Fact.

HAROLD "DUSTY" MILLER

Dusty Miller was born in Liverpool in 1898, the youngest of nine children. As a boy he showed early artistic promise but the family's financial situation deprived him of an art school education. Nevertheless, he became a very talented, self-taught artist, maintaining a lifelong passion for art in all its forms. After service in the trenches in the Great War, he returned to civilian life and became a Liverpool policeman. In 1926, Dusty married a Manx girl, Freida Caley, and they decided to live in the Isle of Man where he soon fell in love with the Island.

From the early '30s until his death in 1964, Dusty worked initially for the *Isle of Man Examiner* and then for the *Weekly Times*. Over those years, and in addition to his full-time job there, Dusty produced a variety of pen and ink cartoon drawings which became a regular feature of the newspapers; indeed, for many readers, an essential feature. His drawings, frequently with tongue-in-cheek commentary, covered a huge range of subjects - humorous/factual/satirical/caricature and. particularly, political (usually "gentle" but often very hard-hitting).

However, Dusty is perhaps most widely known and remembered for his earliest published drawings, which first appeared in the *Examiner* in the '30s under the banner "It's A Fact". Inspired by a noted American artist of that time, Dusty collected short - and sometimes tall - stories from all corners of the Island covering curious, quirky and downright bizarre subject matters. These became so popular that they were published in a book in 1937 and again, with additions, in 1949. It has been out of print for many years.

In addition to his cartoons, Dusty was an accomplished artist in oils, watercolour and pastels, becoming a founder member of the Isle of Man Art Society in 1953. His untimely death left a great gap in the lives of his family and deprived the Island of a talented, albeit adoptive, Manxman. In response to many requests over the intervening years, the family has now decided to republish Dusty's "It's A Fact" drawings and short stories.

"IT'S A FACT" by DUSTY.

£5 25265.
Nº 153.

Douglas
ISLE OF MAN COMMERCIAL BANKING Cº

I Promise to Pay Bearer

Five

BARGAIN NOTE

UNTIL 1850 IT WAS A GENERAL MANX CUSTOM FOR THE BUYER OF AN ARTICLE, TO TEAR IN TWO PIECES, A BANKNOTE, OF THE VALUE OF THE ARTICLE BOUGHT, GIVE ONE HALF TO THE SELLER, AND RETAIN THE OTHER HALF UNTIL HE HAD TESTED HIS PURCHASE,

THE SECOND HALF OF THE NOTE WAS THEN HANDED OVER TO COMPLETE THE DEAL.

BARGAIN STONE

ANOTHER CUSTOM OF AN EARLIER PERIOD BUT USED MOSTLY AT THE FAIRS, WAS FOR THE SELLER TO THRUST HIS HAND THRO' A STONE (CARVED FOR THE PURPOSE) & WHEN THE BUYER CLASPED THAT HAND, THE BARGAIN WAS STRUCK

SECRECY & DELICACY

STILL IN USE IN SOME MANX CHURCHES; ARE THE LONG HANDLED OFFERTORY PLATES OR BOXES, WHEN THESE ARE PASSED AMONG THE CONGREGATION, THE RICH MAN MAY DROP IN HIS POUND OR THE WIDOW HER MITE, WITHOUT THEIR NEIGHBOURS BEING THE WISER.

"IT'S A FACT" by DUSTY

FAME

"JEFF" THE POOR LITTLE SPOOK OF OBSCURE DALBY HAS BECOME SO FAMOUS, THAT HE WAS RECENTLY QUOTED IN A HIGH COURT ACTION BETWEEN TWO HEADS OF ENGLANDS GREATEST CORPORATION. THE B.B.C.

HUNT THE WREN

WE HAVE IN DOUGLAS, THE ONLY OR BUILDING, IN GREAT BRITAIN OFFICIALLY NAMED AFTER THE KING CROWNED. WHO WAS NOT PUBLIC WORK WHICH IS

FOR MANY YEARS & UNTIL RECENTLY, ON DEC. 26TH A WREN WAS CAUGHT & KILLED, AT DAWN,

Souvenir

KING EDWARD VIII PIER
OPENED BY
THE RT. HON. SIR JOHN SIMON
P.C., G.C.S.I., K.C.V.O., O.B.E., K.C., M.P.
MAY 23RD 1936.

IT WAS CARRIED FROM HOUSE TO HOUSE IN A PROCESSION OF MEN OR BOYS. IN EXCHANGE FOR FOOD OR COIN, ITS FEATHERS WERE GIVEN AS CHARMS TO WARD OFF EVIL. THE NAKED BODY WAS LATER BURIED IN A CHURCHYARD TO THE SINGING OF DIRGES.

In 1935, work was well under way in the building of the new King Edward Pier and cranes and other heavy equipment utilised in the construction can be seen centre left of the view. The Pier was completed and opened for use in May the following year ahead of schedule. The "Edward Pier", as it is now more commonly known, has played an important part in the development of the Port of Douglas ever since its introduction.

"IT'S A FACT" by DUSTY.

LARGEST & SMALLEST

PENKNIVES, ONE A QUARTER OF AN INCH ($\frac{1}{4}$") THE OTHER 4'-4" IN LENGTH, ARE IN POSSESSION OF A DOUGLAS MAN, & MAY BE SEEN IN A SHOP WINDOW ON THE NORTH QUAY.

"WELL, WELL"

ONE OF DOUGLAS'S EARLY VILLAGE PUMPS NOW IN THE GUISE OF A WELL, IS STILL IN FULL DAILY USE IN S. DOUGLAS

SUCCULENT MORSELS

PETER HENRY JOS. BAUME, AN OLD MANX RECLUSE & ALLEGED REFUGEE FROM THE FRENCH ROYAL COURT, WHO LIVED ON THE 5TH QUAY DOUGLAS,

HAD A STANDING ORDER WITH THE BOYS OF THE NEIGHBOURHOOD, FOR FROGS AT 3^{D} AND SNAILS AT 2^{D} per can. THESE WERE CAUGHT FOR HIM AT THE NUNNERY, & EATEN 'FRENCH FASHION.'

"IT'S A FACT" by DUSTY.

THE STEPS OF ST. PAULS CATHEDRAL, LONDON. RESTING PLACE OF ENGLAND'S NATIONAL HEROES, WERE MADE OF BLACK MARBLE FROM POOIL-VAISH. ISLE OF MAN

"REMEDY WORSE THAN THE DISEASE."

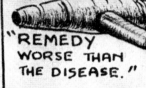

AS RECENTLY AS 1870 THIS TOOTH EXTRACTOR WAS IN USE IN I.O.M.

"OUR QUOTA"

"EARLY SUFFRAGE"

SOUTH SIDE WIVES GAINED THE PRIVILEGE OF DISPOSING IN THEIR WILLS, OF HALF THE JOINT PROPERTY OF THEIR HUSBANDS & THEMSELVES, WHILST THE HUSBAND WAS STILL ALIVE. BY HELPING THEIR HUSBANDS ON THE DAY OF BATTLE.

"IT'S A FACT" by DUSTY.

STONE ½ STONE

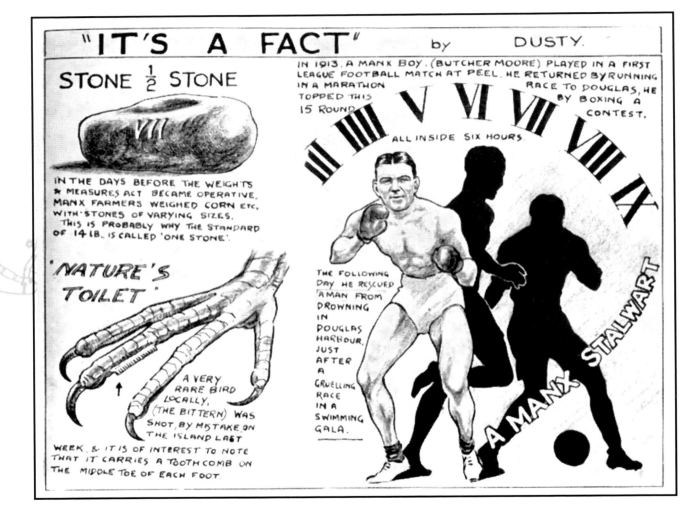

IN THE DAYS BEFORE THE WEIGHTS & MEASURES ACT BECAME OPERATIVE, MANX FARMERS WEIGHED CORN ETC, WITH STONES OF VARYING SIZES. THIS IS PROBABLY WHY THE STANDARD OF 14 LB. IS CALLED 'ONE STONE'.

'NATURE'S TOILET'

A VERY RARE BIRD LOCALLY, (THE BITTERN) WAS SHOT, BY MISTAKE, ON THE ISLAND LAST WEEK, & IT IS OF INTEREST TO NOTE THAT IT CARRIES A TOOTH COMB ON THE MIDDLE TOE OF EACH FOOT.

IN 1913, A MANX BOY, (BUTCHER MOORE) PLAYED IN A FIRST LEAGUE FOOTBALL MATCH AT PEEL, HE RETURNED BY RUNNING IN A MARATHON RACE TO DOUGLAS, HE TOPPED THIS BY BOXING A 15 ROUND CONTEST.

ALL INSIDE SIX HOURS.

THE FOLLOWING DAY HE RESCUED A MAN FROM DROWNING IN DOUGLAS HARBOUR, JUST AFTER A GRUELLING RACE IN A SWIMMING GALA.

A MANX STALWART

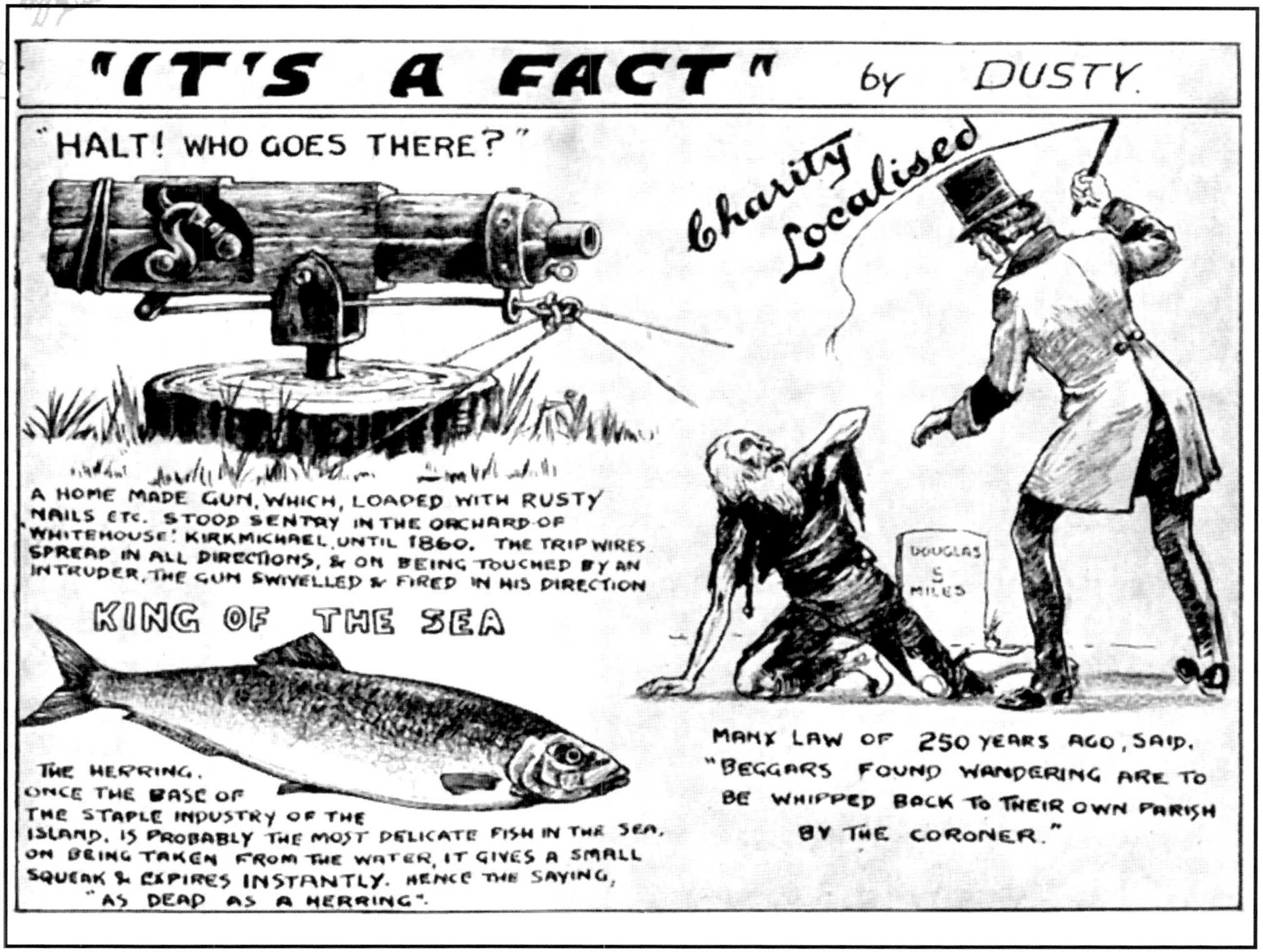

"IT'S A FACT" by DUSTY.

"HALT! WHO GOES THERE?"

A HOME MADE GUN, WHICH, LOADED WITH RUSTY NAILS ETC. STOOD SENTRY IN THE ORCHARD OF WHITEHOUSE! KIRKMICHAEL, UNTIL 1860. THE TRIP WIRES SPREAD IN ALL DIRECTIONS, & ON BEING TOUCHED BY AN INTRUDER, THE GUN SWIVELLED & FIRED IN HIS DIRECTION

KING OF THE SEA

THE HERRING.
ONCE THE BASE OF
THE STAPLE INDUSTRY OF THE
ISLAND, IS PROBABLY THE MOST DELICATE FISH IN THE SEA.
ON BEING TAKEN FROM THE WATER, IT GIVES A SMALL
SQUEAK & EXPIRES INSTANTLY. HENCE THE SAYING,
"AS DEAD AS A HERRING".

Charity Localised

DOUGLAS 5 MILES

MANX LAW OF 250 YEARS AGO, SAID,
"BEGGARS FOUND WANDERING ARE TO
BE WHIPPED BACK TO THEIR OWN PARISH
BY THE CORONER."

13

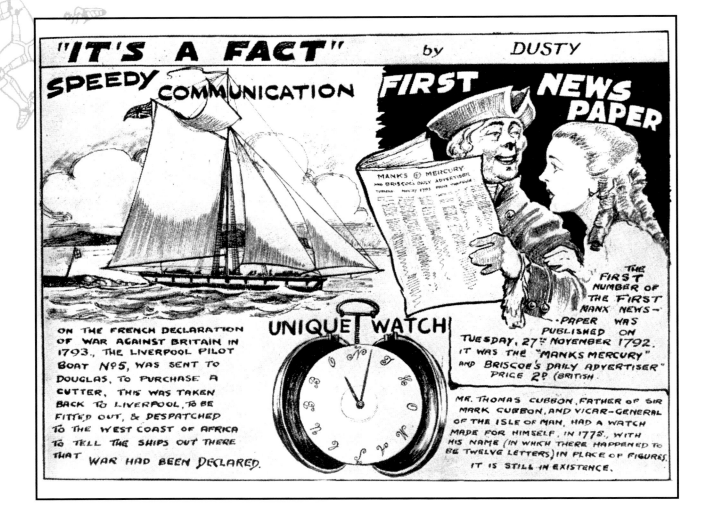

"IT'S A FACT" by DUSTY

SPEEDY COMMUNICATION

FIRST NEWS PAPER

ON THE FRENCH DECLARATION OF WAR AGAINST BRITAIN IN 1793, THE LIVERPOOL PILOT BOAT N°5, WAS SENT TO DOUGLAS, TO PURCHASE A CUTTER. THIS WAS TAKEN BACK TO LIVERPOOL, TO BE FITTED OUT, & DESPATCHED TO THE WEST COAST OF AFRICA TO TELL THE SHIPS OUT THERE THAT WAR HAD BEEN DECLARED.

UNIQUE WATCH

THE FIRST NUMBER OF THE FIRST MANX NEWS-PAPER WAS PUBLISHED ON TUESDAY, 27th NOVEMBER 1792. IT WAS THE "MANKS MERCURY" AND "BRISCOE'S DAILY ADVERTISER" PRICE 2d (BRITISH.

MR. THOMAS CUBBON, FATHER OF SIR MARK CUBBON, AND VICAR-GENERAL OF THE ISLE OF MAN, HAD A WATCH MADE FOR HIMSELF, IN 1775, WITH HIS NAME (IN WHICH THERE HAPPENED TO BE TWELVE LETTERS) IN PLACE OF FIGURES. IT IS STILL IN EXISTENCE.

HERE IS THE NEWS - 1792

reports . . .

ISLAND'S FIRST NEWSPAPER

"Publishing of the Isle of Man's first newspaper has been started. It is known as the *Manks Mercury and Briscoe's Douglas Advertiser*. A spokesman said today they believed they could expect good circulation because of the Island's rapidly increasing population. The latest census results show that there are now just under 28,000 people living in the Island altogether, most of them in the rural areas. The number of people living in the towns is only 7,200 - and most of them are in Douglas, which has now grown to be much larger than the capital, Castletown."

(The report's rather sceptical tone concerning the success of the newspaper was well-founded. The Manks Mercury ceased publication two years later.)

"IT'S A FACT" by DUSTY.

A COVER NOTE

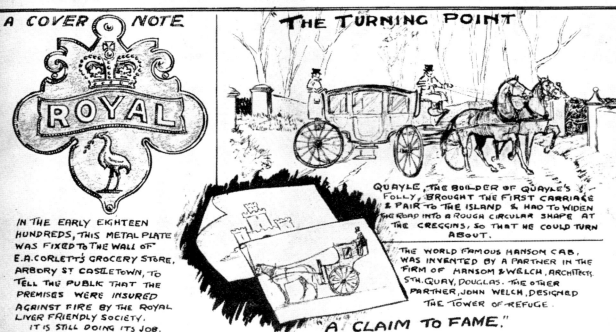

IN THE EARLY EIGHTEEN HUNDREDS, THIS METAL PLATE WAS FIXED TO THE WALL OF E.A. CORLETT'S GROCERY STORE, ARBORY ST CASTLETOWN, TO TELL THE PUBLIC THAT THE PREMISES WERE INSURED AGAINST FIRE BY THE ROYAL LIVER FRIENDLY SOCIETY. IT IS STILL DOING ITS JOB.

THE TURNING POINT

QUAYLE, THE BUILDER OF QUAYLE'S FOLLY, BROUGHT THE FIRST CARRIAGE & PAIR TO THE ISLAND & HAD TO WIDEN THE ROAD INTO A ROUGH CIRCULAR SHAPE AT THE CREGGINS, SO THAT HE COULD TURN ABOUT.

THE WORLD FAMOUS HANSOM CAB, WAS INVENTED BY A PARTNER IN THE FIRM OF HANSOM & WELCH, ARCHITECTS, STH. QUAY, DOUGLAS. THE OTHER PARTNER, JOHN WELCH, DESIGNED THE TOWER OF REFUGE.

"A CLAIM TO FAME."

"IT'S A FACT" by DUSTY.

GENERAL THOS. CUSTINE, WHEN A YOUTH JOINED THE 'KING'S OWN' ENGLISH REGT.. AS A SERGT. HE CAME TO THE ISLAND ON LEAVE, WHEN ABOUT TO BE ARRESTED AS A DESERTER, HE ESCAPED TO DUNKIRK, JOINED THE FRENCH ARMY & ROSE TO THE RANK OF GENERAL. HE COMMANDED THE ARMY WHICH DEFEATED THE PRUSSIANS AT MENTZ. THIS GREAT GENERAL WAS BORN AT LONAN I.O.M.

A PERFECT SPECIMEN OF 'MANX RAT.' BORN IN WALPOLE AVENUE, IT WAS SENT TO THE LIVERPOOL MUSEUM, WHERE IT WAS EXAMINED BY MR. GUTMORE, WHO PRONOUNCED IT AS HAVING NO VESTIGE OF A TAIL.

KISSACKS COTTAGE AT JURBY, WHERE THE TUNE 'RAMSEY TOWN' WAS FOUND.

"IT'S A FACT" by DUSTY

ACCORDING TO OLD MANX LAW, WHEN A MAN WAS GUILTY OF AN OFFENCE AGAINST A MAIDEN, SHE HAD THE CHOICE OF HIS DEATH BY ROPE OR SWORD, OR OF GIVING HIM A RING IN MARRIAGE. ON ONE CLASSIC OCCASION, THE LADY ORDERED THE MISCREANT TO BE HUNG. ON SEEING HIM STRUNG UP, HOWEVER, SHE RELENTED & OFFERED HIM THE RING. HE TOOK THE RING & WITH THE WORDS "ONE CRIME ONE PUNISHMENT" THE HEARTLESS FELLOW DEPARTED.

"Our Gordon"

HE KEPT HIS HEAD

IT IS NOT GENERALLY KNOWN, THAT GORDON HARKER, FAMOUS BRITISH STAGE & FILM STAR, ATTENDED RAMSEY GRAMMAR SCHOOL DURING HIS SCHOOL DAYS

THEIR MAJESTIES
KING EDWARD VII
QUEEN ALEXANDRA
AND HER ROYAL HIGHNESS
PRINCESS VICTORIA
PASSED THROUGH THIS
KELLIA ABBEY QUARTER
XXVVIIIMCMII

SULBY LANDMARK

A VERY FINE PLAQUE BY ARCHIE KNOX, THE WELL KNOWN MANX ARTIST IS WELL HIDDEN AWAY ON THE WALL AT THE END OF THE SULBY STRAIGHT. IT COMMEMORATES THE ROYAL VISIT TO SULBY IN 1902.

THE 1902 ROYAL VISIT

Rumour had it that King Edward VII had visited the Isle of Man incognito on a number of occasions but his visit with Queen Alexandra in 1902 came as a complete surprise.

The royal couple had been cruising aboard their yacht the *Victoria and Albert* when they decided to visit the Island.

The yacht was accompanied by three Royal Navy vessels and caused consternation when the flotilla suddenly appeared in Douglas Bay on 24 August.

Speaker of the House of Keys, A. W. Moore, raced to the harbour and chartered a small boat so that he could be permitted to board the royal yacht and officially welcome the royal visitors to the Island.

The weather was not too good and the sea in Douglas Bay was rather choppy - after due considera-tion it was decided that it would be prudent for the yacht and the royal visitors to steam to Ramsey so that disembarkation could take place at Ramsey's Queen's Pier.

The following day, the King and Queen embarked upon a tour of the Island by carriage and were greeted by large crowds wherever they went. Initially taking a westerly route they travelled through Sulby to Bishopscourt where they met Bishop Straton, and then to the grounds of Peel Castle for an *al fresco* lunch. They next visited Cronkbourne, family home of the Speaker of the Keys, for tea and were then driven into Douglas. They travelled to the Promenade where thousands had gathered to welcome them and, at Derby Castle, boarded a saloon car of the Manx Electric Railway for their journey back to Ramsey.

The visit was a memorable occasion made all the more so because it was total-ly unexpected. For the Mayor of Douglas, Alderman Samuel Webb, their Majesty's visit was especially memorable as it became known that he had been present-ed with a Coronation Medal.

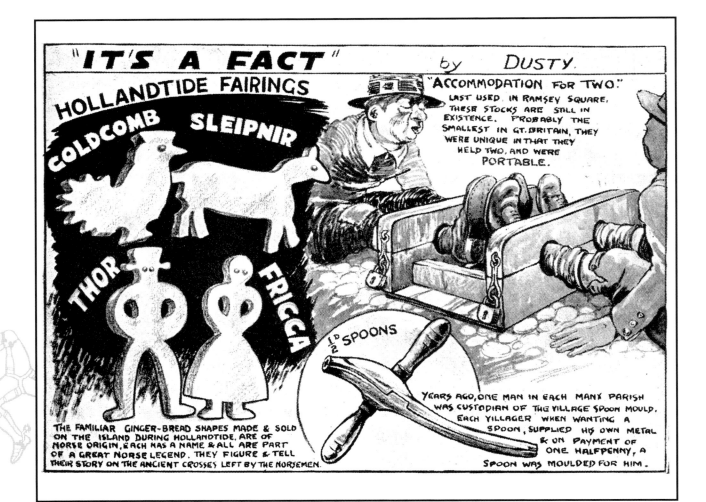

"IT'S A FACT" by DUSTY.

HOLLANDTIDE FAIRINGS

COLDCOMB SLEIPNIR

THOR FRIGGA

THE FAMILIAR GINGER-BREAD SHAPES MADE & SOLD ON THE ISLAND DURING HOLLANDTIDE, ARE OF NORSE ORIGIN, EACH HAS A NAME & ALL ARE PART OF A GREAT NORSE LEGEND. THEY FIGURE & TELL THEIR STORY ON THE ANCIENT CROSSES LEFT BY THE NORSEMEN.

"ACCOMMODATION FOR TWO." LAST USED IN RAMSEY SQUARE, THESE STOCKS ARE STILL IN EXISTENCE. PROBABLY THE SMALLEST IN GT. BRITAIN, THEY WERE UNIQUE IN THAT THEY HELD TWO, AND WERE PORTABLE.

½D SPOONS

YEARS AGO, ONE MAN IN EACH MANX PARISH WAS CUSTODIAN OF THE VILLAGE SPOON MOULD. EACH VILLAGER WHEN WANTING A SPOON, SUPPLIED HIS OWN METAL & ON PAYMENT OF ONE HALFPENNY, A SPOON WAS MOULDED FOR HIM.

"It's a fact" by DUSTY.

"MORE THAN HER BIT"

"KATE CREGEEN"

THE I.O.M.S.P.Co's VICTORIA HOLDS THE PROUD RECORD OF HAVING CARRIED 1,000,000 BRITISH TROOPS TO AND FROM THE BATTLEFIELDS OF EUROPE, DURING THE GREAT WAR 1914—1918.

THERE ARE MORE PEOPLE OF MANX DESCENT, IN CLEVELAND, OHIO U.S.A., THAN THERE ARE IN THE ISLE OF MAN.

CLEVELAND OHIO

ANNY ONDRA, GERMANY'S FILM SWEETHEART, NOW MRS MAX SCHMELING, WIFE OF THE BOXER WHOSE RECENT AMAZING VICTORY OVER JOE LOUIS, HAS BROUGHT HIM SO MUCH IN THE LIMELIGHT, ONCE LIVED ON THE ISLAND & TOOK THE MANX CHARACTER PART OF 'KATE CREGEEN', IN THE 'MANXMAN, WHEN IT WAS FILMED HERE IN 1928

"IT'S A FACT" by DUSTY

GRAYNOGE THE 1ST

THE SCHOONER 'HOOTON' OF GARLIESTON, VOYAGING FROM WHITEHAVEN, WAS WRECKED OFF RUE POINT, ABOUT THE YEAR 1800 ON BOARD SOMEONE HAD A BOX CONTAINING SEVERAL HEDGEHOGS, THESE WERE BROUGHT ASHORE, SOME ESCAPED. THESE WERE THE FIRST ON THE ISLAND. THE MANX NAME FOR THEM, 'GRAYNOGE', MEANS SOMETHING CAUSING HORROR.

G 61A CALLING

"BELIEVE IT OR NOT"

IN 1721 A MANX WOMAN'S LEG FELL OFF BELOW THE KNEE, THE STUMP HEALED & WITHIN A FEW WEEKS SHE WAS QUITE WELL AGAIN. THE WOMAN WAS A MRS. JOUGHIN OF K.K. ANDREAS, AND THE FACT IS VOUCHED FOR BY BISHOP WILSON, IN HIS NOTEBOOK.

THERE IS A WIRELESS BROADCASTING STATION IN DOUGLAS, BUILT BY MR. H. COLEBOURN, IT IS IN DAILY USE, WHEN THE OWNER CONVERSES WITH PLACES AS FAR APART AS EGYPT AND CALIFORNIA. A CONDITION OF HIS TRANSMITTING LICENSE, IS, THAT IN TIMES OF EMERGENCY, HE MUST ALLOW THE GOVERNMENT FULL USE OF THE SET.

"IT'S A FACT" by DUSTY

AS RECENTLY AS 1860, ON THE 4th JULY, MIDSUMMERS EVE, A CART WHEEL BOUND WITH STRAW & TARRED OVER, WAS TAKEN TO A HILLTOP, SET ON FIRE, & TRUNDLED INTO THE VALLEY, AN EXPRESSION OF SUNWORSHIP

"HOUSE OF KEESH"

LHAA BOALDYN (THE DAY OF BAAL'S FIRE)

"A LONG STOCKING"

"SHE'S GOT A LONG STOCKING SOMEWHERE" WAS THE SAYING ORIGINATED BY THE USE OF STOCKING PURSES BY THE MANX-FOLK OF YESTERDAY.

THE NAME 'KEYS' IS DERIVED FROM THE MANKS "KEESH" (A TAX), THE ORIGINAL MEMBERS WERE CALLED "TAXIAXI" AND. WERE HOSTAGES TO THE LORD OF THE ISLE, FOR THEIR DIFFERENT CLANS.

"IT'S A FACT" by DUSTY.

THE WHITE MAN OF EAST BALDWIN

THIS CURIOUS CAIRN ON THE MOUNTAIN TOPS AT ARDERRY, WAS BUILT IN MEMORY OF A DEEMSTER, WHO PERISHED IN A SNOWSTORM WHILST ON AN ERRAND OF MERCY FROM RAMSEY TO CASTLETOWN.

BOX O' DIAMONDS

THIS NICKNAME WAS GIVEN TO MR JOHN FAYLE OF FOXDALE ON ACCOUNT OF HIS BRILLIANT INTELLECT, AND SMALLNESS OF STATURE. HE STOOD 4 FT. 2 INS., PROBABLY THE SMALLEST KNOWN MAN IN THE ISLAND

JOHN WESLEY
1703   1791

WESLEY SPENT HIS FIRST NIGHT ON THE ISLAND, IN A HOUSE IN HOPE ST, DOUGLAS, SO THE OWNER PLACED THIS BUST OF HIM, ON THE ROOF TO COMMEMORATE THE FACT.

IT IS STILL THERE.

HERE IS THE NEWS - 1777

reports . . .

VISIT OF JOHN WESLEY

John Wesley, the leader of the people calling themselves 'Methodists' ended his visit to the Isle of Man today and said the support and encouragement he had received from the Manx People had led him to believe that the Island will be entered as a separate circuit at next year's Wesleyan Conference. He added that he hoped to return to the Island in the near future to see how well his work has made progress. We have this report:

"It now seems that Methodism has gained a strong foothold in the Island after many years of resistance and opposition from the established church. And there is no doubt that it has been the preaching of John Wesley during his visit that has won over many new adherents. It is now nearly 20 years since the first Methodist preacher arrived in the Island. He was John Murlin, known as 'The Weeping Prophet', who arrived at Ramsey and stayed a week. But he departed declaring that he could do no good in what was a nest of smugglers.

Two years ago the Methodist Church in Liverpool sent John Crook to Douglas to pursue the cause and, although he had some success, he also encountered official opposition, and was even offered violence by a mob in Douglas, set on him by the Minister of St Matthew's Church.

There has since been a pastoral letter to the clergy sent out by the Bishop of Sodor and Man condemning the Methodist preachers and their presence in the Island.

But this does not appear to have convinced all the clergy - nor Lieutenant-Governor Richard Dawson. As a result, John Wesley was afforded a genuine welcome when he arrived in Douglas by sailing ship from Whitehaven earlier this week.

During his stay, Wesley preached throughout the Island notably at Castletown - to a huge concourse of people outside Castle Rushen - and at Peel where he preached twice.

The text of the Bishop's pastoral letter on Methodism has just been published in full and it is in severe terms. Bishop Richmond speaks of the "crude, pragmatic and inconsistent, if not profane and blasphemous, extempore effusions of these pretenders to the true religion." He says the clergy should "use their utmost endeavours to dissuade their flock from following or being led and misguided by such incompetent teachers".

"IT'S A FACT" by DUSTY.

THE BIGGEST KNOWN MANXMAN WHO EVER LIVED, JAMES ARTHUR CALEY, OF SULBY, STOOD SEVEN FEET ELEVEN INCHES IN HEIGHT, AND WEIGHED 44 STONES. HE TRAVELLED WITH BARNUM & BAILEY'S CIRCUS IN AMERICA, AND DIED AT THE AGE OF 43 YEARS, FROM SUSPECTED POISONING BY A RIVAL CIRCUS.

(COMPARED WITH A 6ft POLICEMAN)

THE FIRST STEAMSHIP TO SAIL IN MANX WATERS WAS THE "HENRY BELL". SHE HAD A 10 H.P. ENGINE, & HER SPEED WAS NINE KNOTS. BUILT IN 1812, SHE ARRIVED OFF RAMSEY IN JUNE 1815, WHEN A CUTTER MANNED BY SIX EXPERT OARS-MEN, PUT OUT TO SAVE THE CREW, IN THE BELIEF THAT THE VESSEL WAS ON FIRE. ON ARRIVAL AT LIVERPOOL, THE 'HENRY BELL' WAS RECHRISTENED 'ELIZABETH'.

"IT'S A FACT" by DUSTY.

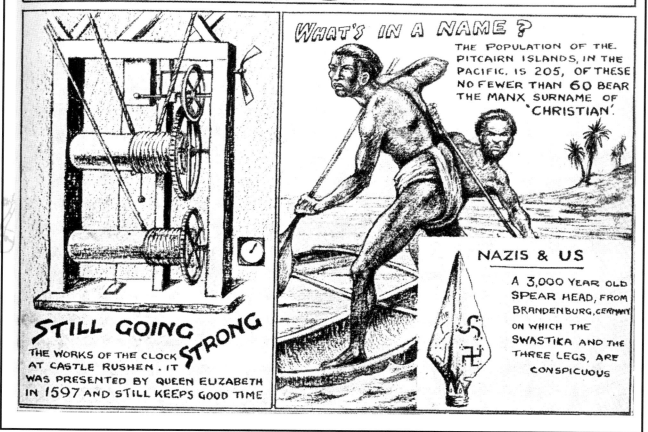

STILL GOING STRONG

THE WORKS OF THE CLOCK AT CASTLE RUSHEN. IT WAS PRESENTED BY QUEEN ELIZABETH IN 1597 AND STILL KEEPS GOOD TIME

WHAT'S IN A NAME?

THE POPULATION OF THE PITCAIRN ISLANDS, IN THE PACIFIC, IS 205, OF THESE NO FEWER THAN 60 BEAR THE MANX SURNAME OF 'CHRISTIAN'.

NAZIS & US

A 3,000 YEAR OLD SPEAR HEAD, FROM BRANDENBURG, GERMANY ON WHICH THE SWASTIKA AND THE THREE LEGS, ARE CONSPICUOUS

27

IT'S A FACT by DUSTY.

SMOKE PENNY

AT ONE TIME EVERY HOUSE THAT HAD A CHIMNEY, WAS TAXED ONE PENNY PER YEAR, THIS WAS KNOWN AS A SMOKE PENNY.

Isle of Sodor?

THE NAME 'SODOR' WAS GIVEN TO PEEL ISLAND, AS BEING THE SEAT OF THE CATHEDRAL OF THE DIOCESE, THE NAME 'MAN' WAS ADDED TO THE TITLE LATER.

MISPLACED SYMPATHY

EIGHT YEARS AGO, THE CREW OF THE PORTERIN LIFEBOAT, SAW A LARGE FIRE AT SEA. ALTHOUGH IT WAS 10.P.M. ON A WINTERS NIGHT, & AN EASTERLY GALE WAS BLOWING, THEY PUT OUT.

WHEN 15 MILES AT SEA, THEY DISCOVERED THAT THE FIRE WAS ON THE MOUNTAINS OF MOURNE, IRELAND.

28

"IT'S A FACT" by DUSTY.

'Och aye'

ALL MANX FISHING VESSELS USED TO PUT A 'LUCK' PENNY BENEATH THE MAST WHEN IT WAS BEING 'STEPPED IN'. PERHAPS THIS ACCOUNTS FOR SO MANY SCOTSMEN SAILING ON MANX BOATS

IMPOSTERS!

ALTHO' THEY ARE PURE RUMPIES, THESE FOWLS ARE NOT MANX NATIVES. THEY ORIGINATE FROM CHILE, S. AMERICA, AND THEY LAY BLUE EGGS

A BEGGAR ON HORSEBACK.

ABOUT 1850, A CRIPPLED BEGGAR WAS IN THE HABIT OF STRUGGLING INTO PEEL EACH DAY. HE WAS SUCH A PAINFUL SIGHT, THAT THE GOOD CITIZENS OF PEEL RAISED A SUBSCRIPTION TO BUY HIM A HORSE.

"IT'S A FACT" by DUSTY.

127 YEARS BEFORE ENGLAND

THE FIRST ENGLISH BRONZE COINS WERE MINTED IN 1860, WHILST THE FIRST MANX BRONZE PENNIES WERE MINTED IN CASTLETOWN IN 1733

"ERIN IN MONA"

FORT ANNE HOTEL IS BUILT ON IRISH SOIL, IMPORTED ABOUT 1790 FOR A BET.

A COOL '50'.

THE FASTER OF THE COMPETITORS IN THE MANX BICYCLE T.T., WHILST DESCENDING THE MOUNTAINS, ATTAIN THE AMAZING SPEED OF 50 M.P.H.

HERE IS THE NEWS - 1765

reports . . .

NEW COINS NOW IN USE

The new issue of Manx coinage is now in general use in the Island and fulfilling the intention that it should, with the remains of the 1733 issue, supplant the use of any other copper coinage from other countries. One of the last acts of the late Second Duke of Atholl was to authorise the issue. It consists of pennies and halfpennies bearing the Ducal crown on one side and the Three Legs of Man on the other. The exchange rate is one of 14 Manx pence to the English shilling. The act providing for the issue says that henceforth, "no person shall be obliged to take any other brass or copper money."
We have this report:

'It will be recalled that James Stanley, tenth and last Earl of Derby, had been so impressed by the first Manx coins issued by Douglas merchant John Murrey as far back as 1668, that he decided to issue his own coinage, which he was prepared to accept as rent. The first of his coins appeared in 1709 and it was not until 1733 that a further issue was produced.

Even then, counterfeiting was prevalent and bartering remained the main currency at markets.

However, the Derby issue had to suffice until the first Atholl coinage appeared as recently as 1758. These were minted in copper by John Florry in Birmingham and consisted of pennies and halfpennies - the same in every way except size.

The obverse side bears the monogram A D (Athol Dux) based on the date and surmounted by a ducal coronet. The reverse has retained the Three Legs and Motto.

It is hoped that these features will be retained when the first of the new regal coins appear.'

| Derby coins, 1709 | Derby coins, 1733 | Atholl coins, 1758 |

IT'S A FACT   by DUSTY.

TOP STOREY

UNDER THE CLIFFS AT MAUGHOLD, CARRION CROWS HAVE BUILT A PILLAR OF NESTS. EACH YEAR THE OLD NEST SOLIDIFIES WITH MUD, BRINE & REFUSE LEFT BY THE BIRDS, AND FORMS A FOUNDATION FOR THE NEW NEST. THE PILLAR IS ABOUT 8 ft. HIGH

"GREAT HARRY"

THERE IS A PROVERBIAL SAYING AMONGST UNITED STATES SAILORS, THAT THE "GREAT HARRY" (BUILT BY HENRY VIII) SWEPT A DOZEN FLOCKS OF SHEEP OFF THE ISLE OF MAN WITH HER BOBSTAY.

GREAT SCOT!

IN THE YEAR 1511, NINE OUT OF TEN OF THE FARMERS, IN THE ISLE OF MAN, HAD THE PREFIX 'MAC' TO THEIR SURNAME.

33

"IT'S A FACT" by DUSTY.

THE BIG SNOW

THE BIGGEST SNOW EVER KNOWN ON THE ISLAND WAS IN FEBRUARY 1895. THE SNOW WAS "12 to 16 feet deep". SOLDIERS FROM CASTLETOWN BARRACKS WERE EMPLOYED DIGGING OUT COTTAGERS

"BEFORE SMEDLEY"

CANNED POTATOES WERE BEING EXPORTED FROM THE ISLE OF MAN, 75 YEARS AGO, BY KING'S OF THE STH QUAY. THEY WERE PACKED IN IRON CANS 3'x 18"x 9" & WERE SENT TO H.M. NAVY & MERCHANT SERVICE.

THE ORIGINAL STONE FROM WHICH DISTANCES OUT OF DOUGLAS WERE MEASURED, STILL STANDS AS A CORNER STONE OF IMPERIAL BUILDINGS NTH QUAY, THE THEN MARKET PLACE OF DOUGLAS.

CASTLETOWN X MILES
PEEL X½ MILES
RAMSEY XVII MILES.

THE ONE BEFORE THE FIRST

HERE IS THE NEWS - 1895

reports . . .

The Isle of Man has been brought to a complete standstill by the worst blizzard in living memory. All roads are impassable, people are trapped in their homes, business life in the towns has been suspended and there are a number of reports of people freezing to death. There has also been at least one ship lost at sea. We have the following report:

'The first week in February will go down in Manx history because of the blizzard which has raged for two days and two nights. It is estimated that at least two feet of snow has fallen and the fierce gales have left drifts up to 14 feet deep in country areas.

All roads and railway lines are blocked and people who have managed to dig their way out of their homes have found commercial life virtually halted.

In Douglas, hardly any shops are open because of 10 foot drifts - and gentlemen like Major Stephen and Major Spittall have been making their way around town in a carriage whose wheels have been replaced by steel runners.

The worst disaster of the blizzard involved the sailing ship 'Nelson Rice' which was driven ashore on the rocks below Douglas Head. All her ship's company are feared drowned.

A vessel also went aground in Ramsey Bay and when the lifeboat put to sea, her crew braving frozen spray and huge waves, they found two men alive after hanging in the rigging all night, sheltering in the belly of the topsail. They had icicles inches long on their faces.

On land, it is reported that Mr Thomas Morris, tenant of the Slieau Lewaigue Hotel, was frozen to death while on his way home. Work on constructing the Snaefell Mountain Electric Railway has been halted and there have also been some narrow escapes for children - one had to be dug out of a drift at Rosemount in Douglas after a hand was seen sticking out of the snow.

At Maughold School most of the children have been marooned since the start of the blizzard, but they are believed to be safe and well in the schoolhouse.

For the moment there is no sign of a thaw and it is forecast that the snow will still be lying in the Island well into March.

Only then will it be possible to assess the trail of damage that has been caused, and the loss of life.'

"IT'S A FACT" by DUSTY

STILL ANOTHER RUMPY.

THE 'LITTLE GREBE' A PERFECT SPECIMEN OF RUMPY WILD BIRD. THOUGH LITTLE KNOWN, IT INHABITS THE ISLE OF MAN.

IN THE 1790's, LORD DERBY BUILT SEVERAL CORN-MILLS ON THE ISLAND, HE THEN SENT HIS SOLDIERS ROUND TO ALL FARMS, TO SMASH EVERY QUERN, THIS WAS TO PREVENT THE FARMERS GRINDING THEIR OWN CORN & TO FORCE THEM TO PATRONIZE DERBY'S MILLS.

THE ONLY ONE NOT SMASHED WAS THE BISHOP'S

EARLY RACKETEER

"Effective!"

WITH EIGHT HEAVY LEATHER THONGS, THIS SPECIALLY DESIGNED SCHOOLMASTER'S PUNISHER, WAS IN UNIVERSAL USE ON MANX SCHOOLBOYS OF A HUNDRED YEARS AGO

"IT'S A FACT by DUSTY.

GOOD OLD DAYS?

BURNING OUT THE 'WITCHES'

AS RECENTLY AS ONE HUNDRED YEARS AGO, MANX FISHERMEN WERE IN THE HABIT OF EXORCISEING THEIR BOATS ON FIRST SIGHT OF THE HERRING. TO DO THIS THEY LIGHTED A FIRE OF DRYLING OR HEATH IN THE BOAT.

AT THE TIME OF SIR JOHN STANLEY (1400) THE TENANTS OF THE ISLAND WERE SO POOR, THAT THEY COULD NOT AFFORD DOORS & WINDOWS TO THEIR HOUSES, BUT FILLED UP THE APERTURES WITH GORSE AND BRIARS.

UNIQUE MEDALLION.

WELTKRIEG 1914-1915 ERINNERUNG AN DIE KRIEGSHAFT DOUGLAS ISLE OF MAN

ENTIRELY WITHOUT ORTHODOX TOOLS, & MADE OF LEADFOIL FROM TEACHESTS, THIS EXQUISITE MEDAL WAS STRUCK BY A GERMAN PRISONER OF WAR AT CUNNINGHAM'S CAMP, 1915. IT IS IN MEMORY OF ALL THE PRISONERS AT DOUGLAS.

"IT'S A FACT" by DUSTY

THE CURSE OF ST. PATRICK

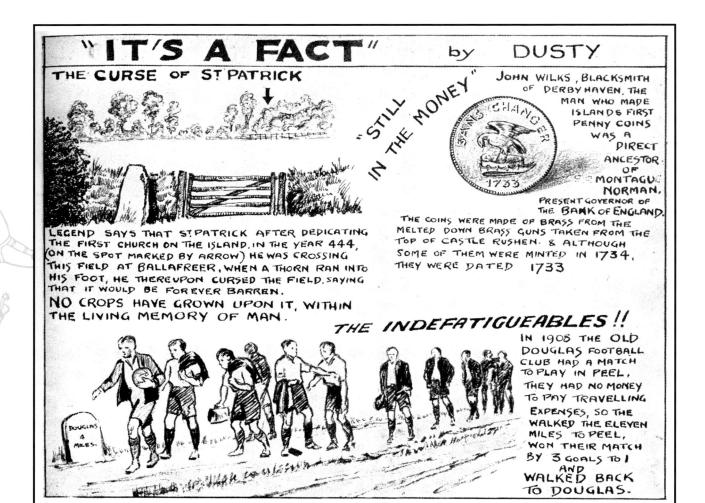

LEGEND SAYS THAT ST. PATRICK AFTER DEDICATING THE FIRST CHURCH ON THE ISLAND, IN THE YEAR 444, (ON THE SPOT MARKED BY ARROW) HE WAS CROSSING THIS FIELD AT BALLAFREER, WHEN A THORN RAN INTO HIS FOOT, HE THEREUPON CURSED THE FIELD, SAYING THAT IT WOULD BE FOREVER BARREN.

NO CROPS HAVE GROWN UPON IT, WITHIN THE LIVING MEMORY OF MAN.

"STILL IN THE MONEY"

JOHN WILKS, BLACKSMITH OF DERBY HAVEN, THE MAN WHO MADE ISLANDS FIRST PENNY COINS WAS A DIRECT ANCESTOR OF MONTAGUE NORMAN, PRESENT GOVERNOR OF THE BANK OF ENGLAND. THE COINS WERE MADE OF BRASS FROM THE MELTED DOWN BRASS GUNS TAKEN FROM THE TOP OF CASTLE RUSHEN. & ALTHOUGH SOME OF THEM WERE MINTED IN 1734, THEY WERE DATED 1733

THE INDEFATIGUEABLES !!

IN 1908 THE OLD DOUGLAS FOOTBALL CLUB HAD A MATCH TO PLAY IN PEEL, THEY HAD NO MONEY TO PAY TRAVELLING EXPENSES, SO THE WALKED THE ELEVEN MILES TO PEEL, WON THEIR MATCH BY 3 GOALS TO 1 AND WALKED BACK TO DOUGLAS.

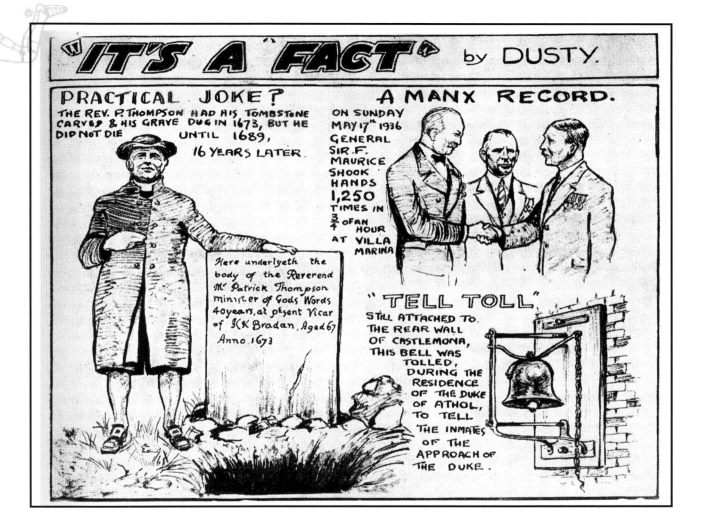

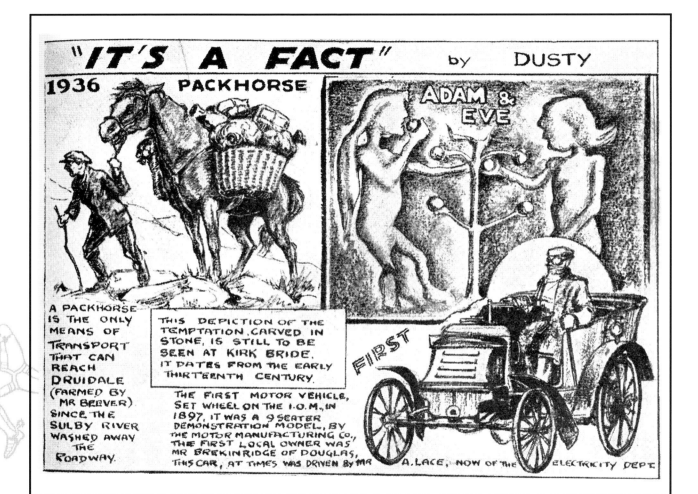

"IT'S A FACT" by DUSTY

1936 PACKHORSE

ADAM & EVE

FIRST

A PACKHORSE IS THE ONLY MEANS OF TRANSPORT THAT CAN REACH DRUIDALE (FARMED BY MR BREVER) SINCE THE SULBY RIVER WASHED AWAY THE ROADWAY.

THIS DEPICTION OF THE TEMPTATION, CARVED IN STONE, IS STILL TO BE SEEN AT KIRK BRIDE. IT DATES FROM THE EARLY THIRTEENTH CENTURY.

THE FIRST MOTOR VEHICLE, SET WHEEL ON THE I.O.M., IN 1897, IT WAS A 9 SEATER DEMONSTRATION MODEL, BY THE MOTOR MANUFACTURING CO., THE FIRST LOCAL OWNER WAS MR BREKINRIDGE OF DOUGLAS, THIS CAR, AT TIMES WAS DRIVEN BY MR A. LACE, NOW OF THE ELECTRICITY DEPT.

40

HERE IS THE NEWS - 1899

reports . . .

APPROVAL FOR MOTOR CARS

Tynwald this year has given approval to a law which permits the new 'horseless carriages' to travel on Manx roads at a maximum speed of 14 miles per hour, thus exempting them from the Highway law for steam rollers which are restricted to 4 miles per hour, with someone walking in front and waving a red flag.

The few owners of a motor car are delighted at the prospect of travelling around the Island at such speeds, though already some have been accused of 'furious driving' which creates clouds of dust and frightens horses.

The 450 operators of horse-drawn carriages have also expressed great alarm at the prospect of losing their livelihood, after the internal combustion engine has already demonstrated it has the power to climb the steepest hills without the assistance of passengers having to push the vehicle.

"IT'S A FACT" by DUSTY.

NO Nº 3

IN THE HEYDAY OF THE PEEL FISHING FLEET, NO BOAT WOULD BE THIRD TO LEAVE THE HARBOUR, SO NUMBERS 3 & 4 SAILED TOGETHER AS ONE

DERELICT TYNWALD

TYNWALD WAS ONCE HELD AT ALGAYRE, NEAR BALDWIN, AND THE SITE IS STILL TO BE SEEN, AFTER LYING UNUSED FOR OVE 500 YEARS.

ORIGIN OF THE T.T.

THE THEN EDITOR OF 'MOTOR CYCLE' GOT THE IDEA FOR A TOURIST TROPHY RACE AFTER SEEING THE GORDON BENNET CAR RACE IN THE ISLE OF MAN. THE FIRST T.T., WAS RUN IN 1907

HERE IS THE NEWS - 1908

reviews the situation . . .

MOTOR RACING

National newspapers which branded the Isle of Man the "Isle of Manslaughter" have been proved scaremongers. The most controversial autocar race ever, preceded by dire warnings of impending disaster, has been held without catastrophe.

The campaign against September's Autocar TT was led by *The Times* of London which argues that the cars had become so powerful that they could wreak havoc among spectators if there were accidents. The campaign's intention was to stop autocar racing over the 37-mile Snaefell Mountain Course.

The Manx authorities dismissed the fears as scaremongering and the RAC decided to press ahead. However, it now seems the RAC will withdraw from organising the event for a while to allow all this scaremongering to die down, and this has the support of the motor manufacturers.

Within the Manx tourist industry this will be a sad blow, though it must be said that the number of spectators arriving here has not matched the predictions which encouraged Tynwald to authorise road closing for the first time in 1904.

Auto-cycle racing, meanwhile, has started to develop a greater appeal. When the A-CU introduced their own trials in 1905, there was only a very limited response, but since the launch of the Auto-Cycle TT in 1907 there has been a greater interest in the two-wheeled sport.

The Auto-Cycle TT causes less inconvenience because it is run over a shorter course, with a start in the centre of St John's. Even this, however, has its critics - some people believe that public roads should not be shut for any reason, and the result is that the roads are not closed for practising and riders have to accept the risk of encountering private traffic.

The motorcycle event is becoming so popular that the course is becoming overcrowded and the A-CU may move the race to the challenging Snaefell Course.

The infamous Devil's Elbow on the St John's course in 1907.

"IT'S A FACT" by DUSTY

SNOW MOUNTAIN
THE CORRECT NAME OF OUR HIGHEST MOUNTAIN IS 'SNÆFELL' COMPOSED OF SNÆ, I.E. SNOW, & FELL, CONTRACTED FROM FIALL, I.E. MOUNTAIN, SO LITERALLY ITS NAME IS SNOW MOUNTAIN.

"CORN SLEDGE"

FIRST STAGE

UP TO THE PRESENT DAY, SLEADS OR SLEDGES ARE IN USE ON THE ISLAND, FOR CARRYING FARM PRODUCE, DOWN STEEP INCLINES, & MOUNTAIN SIDES.

THE FIRST STAGE COACH, WAS INTRODUCED TO THE ISLAND BY WILLIAM DIXON OF THE 'BRITISH HOTEL' DOUGLAS, IN JUNE 1821. IT WAS KNOWN AS THE 'LIGHT POST COACH' 'MAJESTIC', & RAN FROM DOUGLAS TO RAMSEY, PEEL & CASTLETOWN.

44

"IT'S A FACT" by DUSTY.

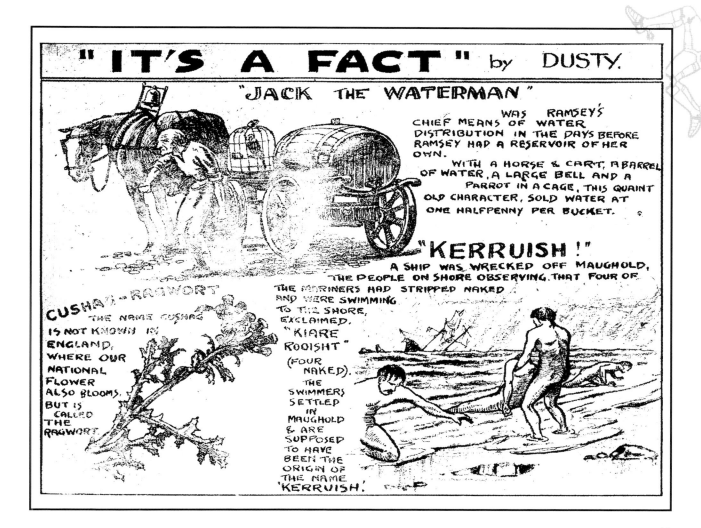

"JACK THE WATERMAN"

WAS RAMSEY'S CHIEF MEANS OF WATER DISTRIBUTION IN THE DAYS BEFORE RAMSEY HAD A RESERVOIR OF HER OWN.

WITH A HORSE & CART, A BARREL OF WATER, A LARGE BELL AND A PARROT IN A CAGE, THIS QUAINT OLD CHARACTER, SOLD WATER AT ONE HALFPENNY PER BUCKET.

"KERRUISH!"

A SHIP WAS WRECKED OFF MAUGHOLD, THE PEOPLE ON SHORE OBSERVING THAT FOUR OF THE MARINERS HAD STRIPPED NAKED AND WERE SWIMMING TO THE SHORE, EXCLAIMED,

"KIARE ROOISHT" (FOUR NAKED).

THE SWIMMERS SETTLED IN MAUGHOLD & ARE SUPPOSED TO HAVE BEEN THE ORIGIN OF THE NAME 'KERRUISH.'

CUSHAG = RAGWORT

THE NAME CUSHAG IS NOT KNOWN IN ENGLAND, WHERE OUR NATIONAL FLOWER ALSO BLOOMS, BUT IS CALLED THE RAGWORT.

"IT'S A FACT" by DUSTY.

STRATEGY

IN THE 1830's TWO RIVAL SHIPS, MONA'S ISLE & ST. GEORGE SET OUT TO RACE TO DOUGLAS, A STRONG SIDE WIND WAS BLOWING, WHICH GAVE THE St. GEORGE A HEAVY LIST & KEPT ONE PADDLE OUT OF THE WATER, CAPT. GILL OF MONA'S ISLE, HOWEVER, HAD HIS CARGO & COAL SHIFTED OVER TO ONE SIDE TO COUNTERBALANCE THE STORM, AND GAINED AN EASY VICTORY.

FARE 6D

ST. GEORGE STEAM PACKET COMP.
27 WATER ST. LIVERPOOL
TICKET - ISSUED AUG 1830
ENTITLED THE PERSON TO TRAVEL PER.
S.S. ST. GEORGE
FROM LIVERPOOL
6D TO DOUGLAS 6D
I.O.M
NOT ADMISSIBLE IN THIS COUNTRY FOR MORE THAN

IN 1830, THE St. GEORGE STEAMPACKET COMPANY OF LIVERPOOL, LOWERED THE SINGLE FARE TO & FROM DOUGLAS TO 6D. THIS RESULTED IN A TERIFFIC INFLUX OF 'MENDICANTS,' BEGGARS, PICKPOCKETS ETC., TO THE ISLAND

OATH STONE

BEFORE THE DAYS OF THE BIBLE (10 CENT.) THE ANCIENT MANKS DID THEIR SWEARING OF OATHS, BY PLACING THE RIGHT FOOT IN A SPECIALLY CARVED STONE, THIS WAS LOOKED UPON AS AN IRREVOCABLE STEP.

46

The 1830s was an important decade in Manx maritime history, in that those years saw the building of the Tower of Refuge in Douglas Bay and the award of the Royal Mail contract to the Mona's Isle Company which promptly changed its name to the Isle of Man Steam Packet Company - both events involved the Liverpool St George Steamship Company . . .

HERE IS THE NEWS 1832

A TOWER OF REFUGE FOR MARINERS

Work has started on building a safe refuge for mariners whose vessels are wrecked on St Mary's Rock in Douglas Bay. It will be a solid stone castellated structure on the rock itself which will provide shelter and also food and water fro shipwrecked men until they can be brought ashore in safety - and it is to be called the Tower of Refuge. We have this report . . .

"The tower, the foundation stone of which was laid on April 23rd this year, is the idea of Sir William Hillary, of Fort Anne, Douglas, who was one of those who founded the RNLI eight years ago. Sir William has long been convinced that such a shelter should be built in view of the number of vessels that have been wrecked on St Mary's Rock, including the Royal Mail Packet "St George" (owned by the Liverpool St George Steamship Company) two years ago. He led the raising of the money by public subscription to pay for it, realising a total of £254/12 shillings. The list is led by the Isle of Man Harbour Commissioners, who contributed £75, the Steam Packet Company and the Laxey and Foxdale mining companies, followed by many family names of distinction in the Island, including the Tobins, the Bacons, the Cosnahans, the Drinkwaters, the Forbes, the Genestes, the Harrises, the Heywoods and the Spittalls, as well as the Quayles of Bridge House, Castletown. There was also a contribution from Mr John Quane, of Ballapaddag in Braddan, whose family have owned St Mary's Rock for many years. Sir William and his family gave £8 and will also meet the £73/6s due to the builders and the architects of what is going to be a substantial structure, designed to brave the elements for a great many years. The architect is Mr John Welch. The Tower of Refuge will be a great contribution to maritime safety in Douglas, along with the plans to build a new lighthouse this year on Douglas Head. The Harbour Commissioners believe the next step should be the building of a breakwater to provide more shelter for Douglas harbour from the south-east. This matter is to be taken up with the British Treasury."

THE ROYAL MAIL

By the end of the 1820s it seemed clear to the business community, indeed to the population as a whole, that the only way to secure a reliable [mail] service was to have, as it was put at the time, 'a Manx company with a Manx steamer and Manx crew.' In 1830 this happy state came about with the Mona's Isle Company, formed by a local syndicate, ordering the first of its steamers, the *Mona's Isle*. The new ship was placed in the hands of William Gill from Glen Auldyn, near Ramsey. He had gone to sea as a lad and rose to command sailing ships like the *Duchess of Atholl* and the *Douglas* which traded between Douglas and Liverpool. He was renowned for his seamanship and knew the treacherous sands of the Mersey like the back of his hand. Now in command of the *Mona's Isle,* he charted the standard route through the sands, now known as the Victoria Channel. The dramatic events of mid-August of that year will be remembered vividly. The *Mona's Isle* took on the *Sophia Jane* of the Liverpool St George Company on the sail to and from Liverpool and beat her handsomely. A month later she took on the flagship of the Liverpool company, the *St George,* and beat her too. The disastrous wreck of the *St George* on Conister Rock confirmed the downfall of the Liverpool St George Company and, a year later, the Mona's Isle Company, which changed its name to the Isle of Man Steam Packet Company in 1832, was awarded the mail contract and an enormous sense of triumph swept the Island. Two mails a week in summer, one in winter, sub-post offices at Castletown, Peel and Ramsey, opened up a new era . . .

THREE LEGS OF MAN

The Three Legs was adopted as the national symbol of the Isle of Man to replace the ship design of Norse times. Its introduction is attributed to Alexander III of Scotland, who gained control of the Island after the death of King Magnus in 1265, and the transfer of the overlordship from Norway to Scotland. Alexander's wife was sister to the King of Sicily, where the three-legged version of the sun symbol had been adopted many years earlier. The Three Legs appear on the Manx Sword of State traditionally said to have been used by Olaf Godredson in the early part of the 13th century, but in reality probably dating from the 14th century. Early representations appear on the 14th century Maughold Cross. It was also during the 14th century that the Legs first appeared both armoured and spurred. In all the above cases, the Three Legs are seen running clockwise (i.e. 'sunwise') and, while there are many later cases using the opposite direction, it is the earlier version that has been adopted in official Government circles. A later addition, appearing for the first time on the first Manx coins issued by John Murrey in 1688, was the Latin motto *Quocunque Gesseris Stabit* (later corrected to *Quocunque Jeceris Stabit*) meaning 'It will stand whichever way you throw it'. The modern coat of arms of the Isle of Man shows the Three Legs surmounted by a crown and supported by a peregrine falcon and a raven, both birds being chosen because of their historical significance.

Source:
*An Illustrated Encyclopedia
of the Isle of Man*

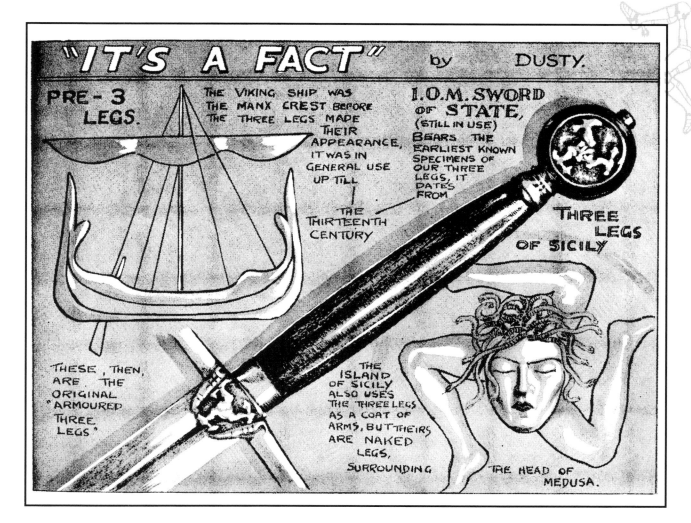

"IT'S A FACT" by DUSTY.

PRE - 3 LEGS.

THE VIKING SHIP WAS THE MANX CREST BEFORE THE THREE LEGS MADE THEIR APPEARANCE, IT WAS IN GENERAL USE UP TILL THE THIRTEENTH CENTURY

I.O.M. SWORD OF STATE, (STILL IN USE) BEARS THE EARLIEST KNOWN SPECIMENS OF OUR THREE LEGS, IT DATES FROM

THREE LEGS OF SICILY

THESE, THEN, ARE THE ORIGINAL "ARMOURED THREE LEGS"

THE ISLAND OF SICILY ALSO USES THE THREE LEGS AS A COAT OF ARMS, BUT THEIRS ARE NAKED LEGS, SURROUNDING

THE HEAD OF MEDUSA.

"IT'S A FACT" by Dusty

NO SNAKES ON THE ISLAND?
AND YET A GRASS SNAKE 18 INS LONG WAS FOUND IN THE GROUNDS OF THE NUNNERY IN 1927

THE LAST OF REYNARD
JOHN FARRANT ESQ. OF BALLAKALLINGHAN, SHOT A WILD FOX AT LEZAYRE IN NOVEMBER 1861, IT WAS SUCH A CURIOSITY THAT IT WAS STUFFED AND EXHIBITED IN A SHOP WINDOW IN RAMSEY.

"LEGEND"
THE KEY OF ST. TRINIANS, CROSBY, & THE SCISSORS WITH WHICH THE TAILOR WAS CUTTING THE PANTS WHEN THE BUGGANE APPEARED, ARE STILL PRESERVED & MAY BE SEEN AT THE 'HIGHLANDER' INN, CROSBY.

51

"IT'S A FACT" by DUSTY.

PRE-PIER

THE ENTRANCE TO DOUGLAS HARBOUR, WAS LIGHTED BY A LANTERN ON A POLE, IN THE DAYS BEFORE THE PIER WAS BUILT (1794).

IT WAS THE BLOWING DOWN OF THIS CONTRAPTION THAT CAUSED THE HERRING FLEET DISASTER.

Manx Quads

QUADRUPLETS WERE BORN TO A YOUNG WOMAN IN CASTLETOWN DURING THE EARLY PART OF THE NINETEENTH CENTURY. THEY DID NOT SURVIVE VERY LONG, AND WERE ALL BURIED IN ONE GRAVE.

"The CART before the HORSE"

THIS METHOD OF CARTING MAY STILL BE SEEN ON MOUNTAIN SIDE NEAR CROSBY.

IT'S A FACT by DUSTY.

THE WHITE LADY

THE WHITE LADY OF BALLAFREER AROUND WHICH, MANY LEGENDS ARE WOVEN, IS IN REALITY A PRE-CHRISTIAN GOD, WORSHIPPED PROBABLY 2,000 YEARS AGO, AND STILL IN GOOD PRESERVATION

SAMUEL ALLY AN AFRICAN AND NATIVE OF ST HELENA DIED 1822 AGED 18 YRS BORN IN SLAVERY ERECTED BY A GRATEFUL MASTER

IN BRADDAN CEMETERY LIES THE BODY OF AN AFRICAN NEGRO, BROUGHT FROM SLAVERY AND LAID TO REST BY A MANXMAN, MARK WILKS, GOVERNOR OF ST. HELENA, CUSTODIAN OF NAPOLEON BONAPARTE, WHO CLAIMED THE SLAVE AS A FRIEND AS WELL AS A SERVANT.

GRAVE OF A SLAVE

MINIATURE MENAI

GLEN HELEN, WHICH IS NAMED AFTER HELEN MARSDEN, DAUGHTER OF THE ORIGINAL OWNER, HAS A BRIDGE, BUILT AS A MINIATURE REPLICA OF THE GREAT MENAI BRIDGE

CORNELIUS SMELT

CORNELIUS SMELT was Lieutenant-Governor of the Isle of Man from 1805 until 1832. He was the first Lieutenant-Governor appointed by the Crown during the period when the Duke of Atholl was Governor-in-Chief. The Duke made attempts to oust Smelt but the Home Secretary refused to support him. The Duke introduced harsher measures in the the Isle of Man but Smelt countered the Duke's disfavour with discretion and maintained his personal popularity for over 20 years. He died in 1832 at the age of 85 years and was buried in St Mary's Church, Castletown. However his body was moved to Onchan churchyard when St Mary's Church was converted into offices in the 1980s.

The memorial which stands opposite to the building which was St Mary's Church in the Parade, Castletown was erected in his memory. It was designed by Sir William Hillary and drawn up by John Welch. It takes the form of a Doric column but the original intention to surmount the column with a statue of Smelt could not be completed due to lack of funds.

THE DERBY

The world-famous Derby horserace originated on the Isle of Man. It was inaugurated by the Earl of Derby on 28 July 1627 and was run at Langness in an area still known as 'The Racecourse'. The race was transferred to Epsom in 1779.

Source:
An Illustrated Encyclopedia
of the Isle of Man

"IT'S A FACT" by DUSTY.

The Phantom Statue

THE COLUMN COMMEMORATING GOV. SMELT IN CASTLETOWN IS 100 YEARS OLD THIS YEAR.

WHEN ERECTED IT WAS TO HAVE A STATUE OF THE GOVERNOR SURMOUNTING IT, BUT THE GOOD PEOPLE OF CASTLETOWN REFUSED TO CONTRIBUTE, SO IT REMAINS VACANT

THE FIRST RACEHORSES IN BRITAIN WERE MANX, & WERE RACED IN THE FIRST DERBY AT RONALDSWAY.

BUSHY-EST BUSH

THIS RHODODENDRON BUSH, WHICH GROWS JUST OUTSIDE UNION MILLS, IS SIXTY YARDS IN CIRCUMFERENCE. IT HAS A SINGLE ROOT, & IS STILL EXTENDING.

"Vel Peccagh s'thie?"

In the 1700's MANX LAW MADE IT A FELONY TO ENTER ANY MAN'S HOUSE WITHOUT FIRST CALLING THREE TIMES "VEL PECCAGH S'THIE"? (IS THERE ANY SINNER WITHIN).

2 STICKS WERE SET CROSSWISE BEFORE THE DOOR & IT WAS A CAPITAL OFFENCE TO REMOVE THE WITHOUT PERMISSION, THIS WAS TO PREVENT ANY PERSON ENTERING WHILST THE TENANT WAS OUT.

GOLF AVIARY

FOUR GENTLEMEN FROM ATHOL STREET WERE RECENTLY PLAYING GOLF ON CASTLETOWN LINKS, & ON THE 16TH HOLE (BOGEY 4) THE FOLLOWING REMARKABLE SCORES WERE MADE BY THEM

No1 4 STROKES — A BOGEY
No2 3 STROKES — A BIRDIE
No3 2 STROKES — AN EAGLE
No4 1 STROKE — AN ALBATROSS.

NOT BY GUM

AN INGENIOUS MANX PRACTICE OF THE DAYS WHEN THE USE OF GUM FOR STICKING ENVELOPES WAS UNKNOWN. A SMALL BISCUIT-LIKE DISC OF 'PULP' WAS DAMPED & PLACED UNDER THE FLAP OF THE ENVELOPE, THE FAMILY SEAL WAS THEN PRESSED HARD OVER THE DISC, THIS SERVED THE DOUBLE PURPOSE OF EMBOSSING A CREST & EFFECTIVELY SEALING THE LETTER.

"IT'S A FACT" by DUSTY.

CENTRAL

CAMPBELL BRIDGE, NEAR ST MARKS, WAS ORIGINALLY BUILT IN 1849 & REBUILT IN 1931.

IT IS EXACTLY
$6\frac{1}{4}$ MILES FROM CASTLETOWN
$6\frac{1}{4}$ MILES FROM PEEL &
$6\frac{1}{4}$ MILES FROM DOUGLAS.

Loughtyn SHEEP ARE

PECULIAR TO THE ISLE OF MAN, THEY ARE A VERY EARLY BREED & WOULD BE EXTINCT EXCEPT FOR THE EFFORTS OF ONE OR TWO FARMERS. THEY HAVE FOUR HORNS AND A GAIT SIMILAR TO A MANX CAT.

AROUND THE WORLD

AT XMAS 1935 A CAKE MADE BY A DOUGLAS CONFECTIONER, WAS SENT TO A SHIP ON THE CHINA STATION, THE SHIP HAD LEFT, & THE CAKE FOLLOWED, DOING A COMPLETE CIRCLE OF THE WORLD IN CHASE, IT ARRIVED BACK IN DOUGLAS & WHEN UNPACKED WAS FOUND IN PERFECT CONDITION, EXCEPT FOR A CHIP OFF THE ICING

THE WOOL IS SNUFF COLOURED AND SO FINE, THAT IT IS RETAINED AND WOVEN INTO CLOTH, USUALLY FOR WEARING BY THE FARMERS OWN FAMILY.

"IT'S A FACT" by DUSTY.

FOR A GOOD HORSE

Creer's Career

ROSS CREER, IS THE ONLY MAN TO SECURE EVERY HONOUR OPEN TO MANX FOOTBALLERS, WITH THE EXCEPTION OF A SCHOOLBOY MEDAL.

THIS JUG, NOW IN THE POSSESSION OF A DOUGLAS FAMILY, & ORIGINALLY WON BY A KARRAN OF MAROWN, WAS GIVEN BY LORD DERBY, FOR THE BEST BRED HORSE RUNNING IN THE DERBY AT DERBYHAVEN, SOME 200 YEARS AGO

THE RACE WAS FIRST STARTED TO ENCOURAGE THE TENANTS OF THE RT HON. LORD DERBY TO BREED GOOD HORSES WITHIN THE ISLE OF MAN.

BETWEEN TWO FIRES

THE CENTRAL HEATING APPARATUS, IN ST LUKES. CHURCH BALDWIN IS BUILT. UPON A TOMBSTONE.

"IT'S A FACT" by DUSTY.

REFLECTED GLORY

GOULDEN
SOPHIA JANE
WHO DIED
22ⁿᵈ APRIL 1910
IN HER 70ᵗʰ YEAR

SOPHIA JANE GOULDEN, THE MOTHER OF MRS. PANKHURST, & GRANDMOTHER OF SYLVIA PANKHURST, THE WORLD FAMOUS PIONEERS OF WOMENS SUFFRAGE, WAS MANX.

HER MAIDEN NAME WAS CRAINE. SHE NOW LIES IN BRADDEN CEMETERY.

THE "FLEA" JUMPS

THE FIRST MANX BUILT AIRPLANE, CARINE'S "FLYING FLEA", TOOK ITS INITIAL TEST FLIGHT IN SEPT., 1936, AT MALEW. THE PILOT ONLY TOOK IT TO A HEIGHT OF 50 FEET, BUT IT BEHAVED WELL IN THE AIR, AND LANDED WITHOUT MISHAP.

DEATH GLOVES

STILL PRESERVED IN CASTLE RUSHEN, ARE THE GLOVES WITH WHICH THE ISLAND'S HANG-MAN USED TO BIND THE HANDS OF HIS VICTIMS. THEY WERE LAST USED LATE IN LAST CENTURY

"IT'S A FACT" by DUSTY

DUMBELL'S DOORS OPEN AGAIN

BACON'S HITCH.

AS A CONSTANT REMINDER OF PRE-MOTOR DAYS, THE HITCHING HOOK USED BY MAJOR BACON, FOR TETHERING HIS HORSE, IS STILL FIRMLY FIXED INTO THE WALL OF HIS OLD STABLE IN St. GEORGES St.

GENUINE ANTIQUE

BUT INTO A PUBLIC HOUSE THIS TIME. THE ORIGINAL DOORS OF DUMBELL'S BANK, WHICH WERE FINALLY CLOSED TO THE PUBLIC IN 1900, NOW ADORN THE FRONT ENTRANCE TO THE 'OLD STRAND HOTEL', STRAND St. THEY ARE COMPLETE WITH COAT OF ARMS, WHICH STRANGELY ENOUGH, INCLUDES A BUNCH OF GRAPES

THE HOLES IN THIS OLD STAIRCASE, WERE MADE BY SEA URCHINS, FOR ALTHO' IT HAS BEEN IN ITS PRESENT POSITION FOR OVER 100 YEARS, IN THE PREMISES OF A STONEMASON IN St. GEORGES St, PRIOR TO THAT, IT WAS PART OF A SUBMERGED WRECK.

HERE IS THE NEWS - 1900

reports . . .

" Saturday 3rd February, 1900 is already being dubbed 'Black Saturday' - one of the blackest days in the Island's history, the memory of which will live on for many years to come. The day the Dumbell Banking Company collapsed brought ruin to all parts of the Island. Families have been left without means, money frozen in accounts; marts and auctions have ceased, tradesmen and farmers bankrupted and clergy reduced to poverty. No fragment of Manx life has escaped the calamitous consequences of the crash of Dumbell's Bank.

The charges of fraud brought against five of the bank officials are due to be heard shortly in the Court of General Gaol. But the man held to be mainly responsible, Alexander Bruce, who was appointed general manager in 1878 by George Dumbell himself, will not be among them. Bruce took to his bed in March and the High Bailiff withdrew the warrant against him on the grounds that his arrest would prove fatal. In fact, the man, once the hero of the Island's commercial life, died on 14th July in his 57th year. His death has produced almost every human emotion in most Manxmen and women - from grief to delight, bitterness to sorrow and satisfaction to sadness.

How did it happen? Dumbell's Bank has been a feature of Manx commercial life for almost half a century, apparently as solid and enduring as the Tower of Refuge. George William Dumbell himself was a businessman, lawyer and politician of towering stature, combining, or so it always seemed, financial commonsense with an imaginative appreciation of the opportunities to be seized on our Island.

Not that he always had it all his own way. In the highly competitive world of banking, he found himself confronted with weighty rivals, of whom the Isle of Man Banking Company Limited (later the Isle of Man Bank) founded in 1865, has proved the most serious.

On the fateful Saturday morning the Bank, in its fine building at the foot of Prospect Hill, stood with its stout wooden doors firmly closed. Notices on the door and side windows gave sparse information. Inside, employees began to attempt to sort out the mess. Outside, the crowd grew worried, frightened and increasingly angry. Gradually it was realised that some 8000 depositors, including Douglas Corporation and several Departments of the Manx Government, were in danger of losing their money and savings, if not all, then savagely reduced."

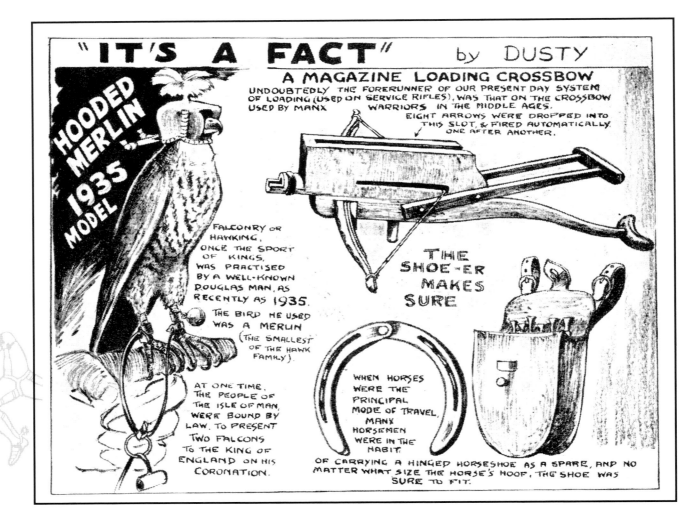

"IT'S A FACT" by DUSTY

A MAGAZINE LOADING CROSSBOW

UNDOUBTEDLY THE FORERUNNER OF OUR PRESENT DAY SYSTEM OF LOADING (USED ON SERVICE RIFLES), WAS THAT ON THE CROSSBOW USED BY MANX WARRIORS IN THE MIDDLE AGES.

EIGHT ARROWS WERE DROPPED INTO THIS SLOT, & FIRED AUTOMATICALLY, ONE AFTER ANOTHER.

HOODED MERLIN 1935 MODEL

FALCONRY OR HAWKING, ONCE THE SPORT OF KINGS, WAS PRACTISED BY A WELL-KNOWN DOUGLAS MAN, AS RECENTLY AS 1935.

THE BIRD HE USED WAS A MERLIN (THE SMALLEST OF THE HAWK FAMILY).

AT ONE TIME, THE PEOPLE OF THE ISLE OF MAN, WERE BOUND BY LAW, TO PRESENT TWO FALCONS TO THE KING OF ENGLAND ON HIS CORONATION.

THE SHOE-ER MAKES SURE

WHEN HORSES WERE THE PRINCIPAL MODE OF TRAVEL, MANX HORSEMEN WERE IN THE HABIT OF CARRYING A HINGED HORSESHOE AS A SPARE, AND NO MATTER WHAT SIZE THE HORSE'S HOOF, THE SHOE WAS SURE TO FIT.

"IT'S A FACT" by DUSTY

DOUGLAS FOUND- -BALTIC BOUND

UP TILL FAIRLY RECENTLY MESSRS. QUALTROUGH OF THE BRIDGE WORKS, WERE BUILDING SHIPS, MOSTLY SCHOONERS. OF ABOUT 150 TONS. THESE VESSELS WERE STOUT ENOUGH TO SAIL, FULLY LADEN, TO PORTS IN THE BALTIC SEA, FROM WHENCE THEY BROUGHT BACK CARGOES OF SILK ETC. THE YARDS ARE NOW GIVEN OVER TO THE MANUFACTURE OF MINERAL WATERS.

TEARE'S MARE. (SKULL)

WHICH, STILL EXISTING IN DOUGLAS, IT WAS FOR MANY YEARS IN THE POSSESSION OF THE LATE MR. TEARE OF BALLAWHANE, IT WAS HIS FRIEND & ADVISER IN ALL HIS TROUBLES, & ALL HIS WISDOM, HE CLAIMED, WAS IMPARTED TO HIM BY THE SKULL THIS WAS AN ACCEPTED FACT IN BALLAWHANE & DISTRICT.

"ARC-VUC-SONNEY" (THE PIG OF PLENTY)

WAS AN APPARITION, PECULIAR TO THE I.O.M, THAT WOULD CROSS A MAN'S PATH ON A MOONLIGHT NIGHT, IT WAS LUCKY TO SEE IT, BUT IF THE MAN WHO SAW IT, WAS LUCKY ENOUGH TO CATCH IT, HIS FORTUNE WAS MADE.

"IT'S A FACT" by DUSTY.

"On the RED PIER"

ODD

THIS PECULIAR LOOKING ODDITY, MAY BE SEEN STRUTTING THE YARD OF THE WHITESTONE INN, BALLASALLA. IT IS HALF TURKEY AND HALF FOWL.

THE OLD RED PIER, IN ITS HEYDAY, WAS SO WELL ESTEEMED AS A PROMENADE, THAT THE PEOPLE WALKING THERE, WERE OBLIGED TO REMOVE THEIR PATTENS (A WOODEN OVERSHOE, MUCH WORN IN THE ISLAND, ABOUT 1820, TO KEEP THE FEET OUT OF THE MUD) FOR FEAR OF SCRATCHING THE PIER SURFACE.

WHISTLING GARGOYLES

LIKE DEFEATED SPIRITS OF EVIL, LEAVING THE CHURCH, THE 8 OPEN MOUTHED GARGOYLES, WHICH ADORN THE STEEPLE OF BUCKS RD CONGREGATIONAL CHURCH, WAIL WITH EVERY PASSING WIND. THIS WEIRD EFFECT IS PROBABLY DUE TO THE PECULIAR DESIGN OF THE MOUTHS.

64

HERE IS THE NEWS - 1801

reports . . .

"Great scenes of jubilation accompanied the official opening of the new pier for Douglas Harbour. The ceremony was led by John, fourth Duke of Atholl, who laid the foundation stone some eight years ago, in 1793, following his appointment as Governor-General. Just about all the town and many from beyond, crowded the harbour to join in the celebrations and take a first walk on the new pier. The pier has been completed at a cost of £22,000 and is an admirable construction which replaces the earlier attempt of building a pier in 1760, which was wrecked in a severe storm.

The architect for the new pier is Mr George Steuart who, as his name suggests, is from Scotland and has long been under the patronage of the Dukes of Atholl. Undoubtedly, Mr Steuart is deserving of high praise and the appearance of Douglas harbour has been greatly enhanced.

Much of the pier and its buildings have been completed in sandstone from Arran, Scotland, a freestone which is readily carved. Because of its reddish hue, the pier is already being called the Red Pier. It is skilfully blended into the North Quay from which it extends a total length of 530 feet thus providing deep water berths at high tide, which means passengers can land for longer periods without being rowed from anchorages in the bay. The pier is 40 feet wide but, after 450 feet, it suddenly expands to 50 feet and is raised 3 or 4 feet above the other. This part is circular in shape, in the centre of which is a handsome lighthouse.

The Red Pier is already proving popular as a promenade and in fine weather is crowded with the genteel, so it is likely to prove the social centre of the town. The pier is neatly paved with flagstones and, in order to preserve its surface, people are being warned not to wear heavy footwear."

"IT'S A FACT" by DUSTY.

The Nun's Seat

"CRYPTIC"?

JUSTLY RESPECTED ARE INTERRED HERE THE REMAINS OF ANN STOWELL ALIAS BROWN WIFE OF THOMAS STOWELL, WHO DIED 17TH JULY 1783 AGED 44 YEARS AND WHO WAS THE MOTHER OF 15 SONS AND ONE DAUGHTER

MAY THEY LIKE HER THEIR TIME EMPLOY AND MEET HER IN THE REALMS OF JOY.

ALONG THE MARINE DRIVE NEAR WALLBERRY BRIDGE, IS THE NUN'S SEAT, WHERE NUNS FROM THE NUNNERY WERE SENT TO DO PENANCE AFTER COMMITTING A MISDEMEANOUR, THEY WERE BIDDEN TO REMAIN IN THIS NATURAL CAVITY IN THE ROCKS, DURING THE RISE OF ONE FULL TIDE. A TERRIFYING EXPERIENCE FOR THOSE GENTLE CREATURES.

"COINCIDENCE"

AN EX-SOLDIER FROM DOUGLAS RECENTLY REVISITED THE BATTLEFIELDS, AND WHILST ON HILL 60, HE FOUND A SHOULDER BADGE OF HIS OLD REGIMENT, THE 8TH. BATT. CITY OF LONDON REGT. THE BATTALION WAS NOT IN ACTION AT HILL 60 AFTER 1916, SO THE BADGE MUST HAVE LAIN BURIED FOR 20 YEARS.

T 8 CITY OF LONDON

THE TOMBSTONE ILLUSTRATED ABOVE, STANDS IN THE CHURCHYARD AT BALLURE, NEAR RAMSEY.

"IT'S A FACT" by DUSTY.

"MOVING DAY"

BY ANCIENT CUSTOMARY LAW, IT WAS PROVIDED, THAT IF ANY ABBEY TENANT DID REMOVE FROM OFF ABBEY LANDS, HE MIGHT BY LAW, TAKE AWAY THE ROOF OF HIS HOUSE, AND ALL DOORS AND WINDOWS.

MIGHTIEST EVER.

THE ISLE OF MAN HAS THE HONOUR OF HAVING POSSESSED THE MOST POWERFUL PADDLE STEAMER THAT EVER FLOATED, THE 'EMPRESS QUEEN.' SHE DEVELOPED 10,000 H.P.

ST. PATRICK'S BED

THE STONE UPON WHICH ST. PATRICK LAY TO REST, WHEN ON THE ISLE OF MAN IN 444 A.D. IS STILL IN ITS ORIGINAL POSITION AT BALLAFREER.

ST JOHN'S WORT

In Manx gaelic: *lus columb killey* is a herb which was traditionally worn for centuries at the Tynwald Ceremony as a symbol of good luck. In the early 19th century this was changed to the more common Mugwort - the *Bollan Bane* in Manx.

THE FAIRY SADDLE

A curiously shaped stone projects from the wall nearly opposite to the entrance to Kirby House in Saddle Road, Braddan. It is said to have been the 'saddle' which the 'little folk' used when they stole the farmers' horses, rode them headlong through the night and returned them to their stables exhausted.

Source:
*An Illustrated Encyclopedia
of the Isle of Man*

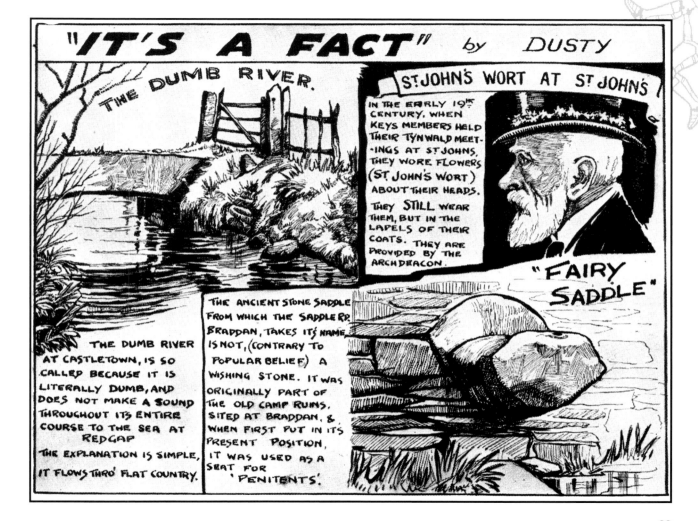

"IT'S A FACT" by DUSTY

THE DUMB RIVER.

ST JOHN'S WORT AT ST JOHN'S

IN THE EARLY 19th CENTURY, WHEN KEYS MEMBERS HELD THEIR TYNWALD MEETINGS AT ST JOHNS, THEY WORE FLOWERS (ST JOHN'S WORT) ABOUT THEIR HEADS.

THEY STILL WEAR THEM, BUT IN THE LAPELS OF THEIR COATS. THEY ARE PROVIDED BY THE ARCHDEACON.

"FAIRY SADDLE"

THE DUMB RIVER AT CASTLETOWN, IS SO CALLED BECAUSE IT IS LITERALLY DUMB, AND DOES NOT MAKE A SOUND THROUGHOUT ITS ENTIRE COURSE TO THE SEA AT REDGAP
THE EXPLANATION IS SIMPLE, IT FLOWS THRO' FLAT COUNTRY.

THE ANCIENT STONE SADDLE FROM WHICH THE SADDLE RD. BRADDAN, TAKES ITS NAME, IS NOT, (CONTRARY TO POPULAR BELIEF) A WISHING STONE. IT WAS ORIGINALLY PART OF THE OLD CAMP RUINS, SITED AT BRADDAN, & WHEN FIRST PUT IN ITS PRESENT POSITION, IT WAS USED AS A SEAT FOR 'PENITENTS'.

"IT'S A FACT" by DUSTY

SWEET LABOUR

"TIME, HERE & THERE"

A UNIQUE SUNDIAL, PROBABLY THE ONLY COMPARATIVE DIAL IN THE WORLD, WAS MADE BY A MANXMAN. IT TELLS THE TIME SIMULTANEOUSLY IN THE I.O.M. & JERUSALEM., I.O.M. & BOSTON. U.SA. I.O.M. & PEKIN. CHINA, AND THE I.O.M & PORT ROYAL JAMAICA.

Jn° Kewley. Ballafleer. Fecit. 1774

WHEN GREAT-GRANDMOTHER WENT OUT TO TEA ON THE ISLAND, SHE WAS FACED WITH QUITE AN OPERATION, BEFORE PUTTING SUGAR IN HER TEA. THE SUGAR WAS IN LARGE PIECES THEN, SO A SUGAR-CUTTER WAS KEPT ON THE TABLE WITH WHICH EACH PERSON CUT HIS OR HER PORTION FROM THE LUMP.

SHELL-LIGHT

THE SCOLLOP SHELL WAS PRESSED INTO LIGHT SERVICE. BY MANXMEN OF 100 YEARS AGO, THE SHELL WAS FILLED WITH TALLOW & A PIECE OF REED DROPPED IN, THUS MAKING A SERVICABLE LAMP.

70

Poachers

ALONG THE MARINE DRIVE, DURING BREEDING SEASON, SEAGULLS WILL SWOOP DOWN, SEIZE YOUNG RABBITS, RISE TO A GREAT HEIGHT, AND DROP THEM ON THE ROCKS BELOW. THEN FOLLOWS A FEED OF GREAT DELICACY, FOR THE SEAGULL.

Economy

AT THE PRINCE OF WALES THEATRE, DOUGLAS, IN JULY 1849. MR J. WOOD, ACTOR, TOOK SIX PARTS IN THE PLAY 'DAY AFTER THE FAIR', HIS WIFE, BEING MODEST, ONLY TOOK THREE.

"GO AND WHISTLE FOR IT"

UP TO 1820, WHISTLING SPOONS WERE IN USE IN THE I.O.M., IF YOU WANTED A SECOND HELPING, YOU RAISED THE SPOON TO YOUR LIPS, AND WHISTLED FOR IT.

DUSTY.

"IT'S A FACT" by DUSTY

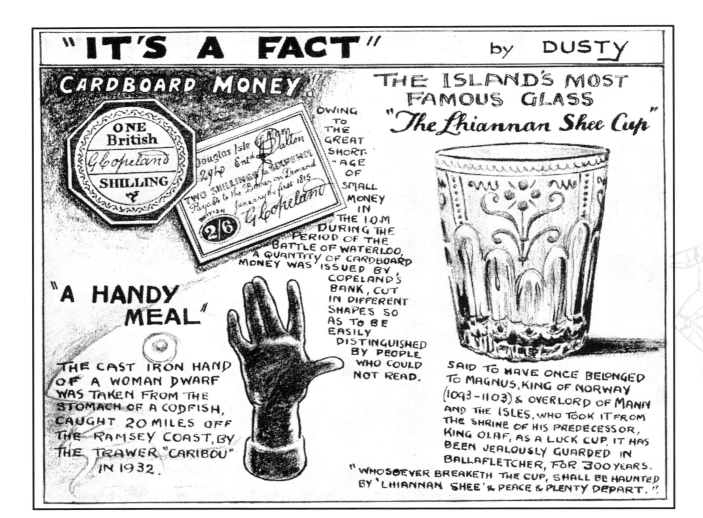

CARDBOARD MONEY!

ONE British G. Copeland SHILLING

Douglas Isle of Man Entd Dalton 29¼p TWO SHILLINGS & SIXPENCE Payable to the Bearer on Demand January the first 1815 BRITISH 2/6 G. Copeland

OWING TO THE GREAT SHORTAGE OF SMALL MONEY IN THE I.O.M DURING THE PERIOD OF THE BATTLE OF WATERLOO, A QUANTITY OF CARDBOARD MONEY WAS ISSUED BY COPELAND'S BANK, CUT IN DIFFERENT SHAPES SO AS TO BE EASILY DISTINGUISHED BY PEOPLE WHO COULD NOT READ.

"A HANDY MEAL"

THE CAST IRON HAND OF A WOMAN DWARF WAS TAKEN FROM THE STOMACH OF A CODFISH, CAUGHT 20 MILES OFF THE RAMSEY COAST, BY THE TRAWER "CARIBOU" IN 1932.

THE ISLAND'S MOST FAMOUS GLASS
"The Lhiannan Shee Cup"

SAID TO HAVE ONCE BELONGED TO MAGNUS, KING OF NORWAY (1093-1103) & OVERLORD OF MANN AND THE ISLES, WHO TOOK IT FROM THE SHRINE OF HIS PREDECESSOR, KING OLAF, AS A LUCK CUP, IT HAS BEEN JEALOUSLY GUARDED IN BALLAFLETCHER, FOR 300 YEARS.

"WHOSOEVER BREAKETH THE CUP, SHALL BE HAUNTED BY 'LHIANNAN SHEE'& PEACE & PLENTY DEPART."

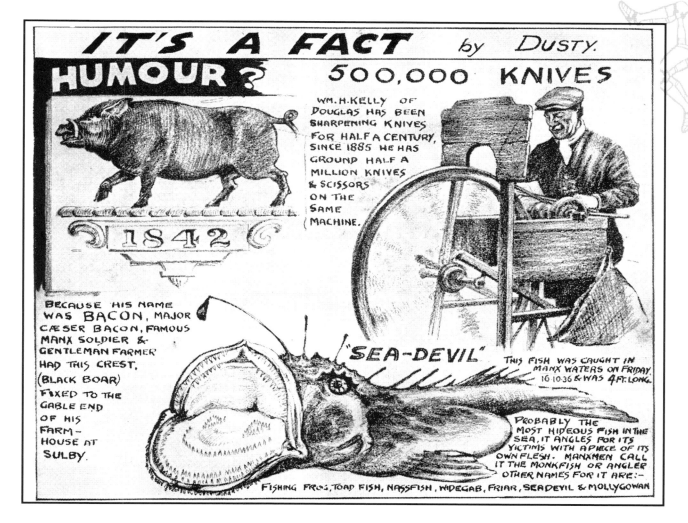

IT'S A FACT by DUSTY.

HUMOUR?

1842

500,000 KNIVES

WM. H. KELLY OF DOUGLAS HAS BEEN SHARPENING KNIVES FOR HALF A CENTURY, SINCE 1885 HE HAS GROUND HALF A MILLION KNIVES & SCISSORS ON THE SAME MACHINE.

BECAUSE HIS NAME WAS BACON, MAJOR CÆSER BACON, FAMOUS MANX SOLDIER & GENTLEMAN FARMER HAD THIS CREST, (BLACK BOAR) FIXED TO THE GABLE END OF HIS FARM-HOUSE AT SULBY.

"SEA-DEVIL"

THIS FISH WAS CAUGHT IN MANX WATERS ON FRIDAY 16·10·36 & WAS 4 FT. LONG.

PROBABLY THE MOST HIDEOUS FISH IN THE SEA, IT ANGLES FOR ITS VICTIMS WITH A PIECE OF ITS OWN FLESH. MANXMEN CALL IT THE MONKFISH OR ANGLER OTHER NAMES FOR IT ARE:—

FISHING FROG, TOAD FISH, NASSFISH, WIDEGAB, FRIAR, SEADEVIL & MOLLYGOWAN

"IT'S A FACT" by DUSTY.

"VICIOUS"
AS LATE AS 1860 MOST ORCHARDS IN THE I.O.M. HAD HUGE MANTRAPS SET. -BIG ENOUGH TO KILL A CHILD.-

'BLISSFUL IGNORANCE'
CAPT. HUGH CROW, OF RAMSEY, IN 1792 ESCAPED FROM A FRENCH PRISON, & WITH A TRICOLOUR COCKADE IN HIS HAT, PASSED HIMSELF OFF AS A BRETON BY ANSWERING ALL QUESTIONS IN MANX.

"?" SET OF TOOLS CARVED ON THE BACK OF A GRAVESTONE, DATED 1765, IN BALLURE CHURCHYARD.

74

"IT'S A FACT" by DUSTY.

DEATHLESS FAME?

COMMEMORATED ONLY BY HIS NAME ON A SMALL MARBLE PLATE, HIDDEN ON THE BACK OF SOMEONE ELSE'S TOMB, WHERE-IN HIS BODY LIES, IS JOHN MARTIN, WHO, TO QUOTE A NEWSPAPER NOTICE CONTEMPORARY WITH HIS DEATH IN 1854, WAS:—— THE GREATEST OF BRITISH ARTISTS & INVENTORS, FAMOUS THE CIVILIZED WORLD OVER, HE DID NOT GO TO GOVERNMENTS, GOVERNMENTS CAME TO HIM; AS TOKENS OF HIS GENIUS, HE HAD PRESENTS FROM KINGS, PRINCES AND NOBLES. THE DEATHLESS NAME OF MARTIN IS ASSOCIATED WITH OUR ISLAND, LIKE THAT OF NAPOLEON WITH ST HELENA. THE GREAT MARTIN.

MISERABLE LOOKING INDEED IS THE NAMEPLATE OF MARTIN, IN A DARK SPOT IN BRADDAN OLD CEMETERY.

STILL RUNNING

A WELL-KNOWN DOUGLAS FIRM HAS A SET OF LEDGERS, IN WHICH THE FIRST ENTRY WAS MADE ON 7TH OCTOBER 1854 — THEY ARE STILL IN USE.

THE BOOKS ARE USE FOR EXPLOSIVES SALES & WHEN THEY WERE FIRST OPENED THERE WERE 37 DIFFERENT MINING COS ON THE ISLAND

FORE-RUNNER OF THE CHURCH ORGAN

KNOWN AS 'THE SERPENT' THESE WEIRD LOOKING MUSICAL INSTRUMENTS WERE EXTENSIVELY USED IN MANX CHURCHES BEFORE THE ADVENT OF THE ORGAN.

THEY ARE NOW OBSOLETE.

HERE IS THE NEWS - 1918

reports . . .

A total of 8,261 men in the Island answered Britain's call to arms, apart from many women who served in the nursing services. Of all Manxmen of military age, 82.3% went to the war - believed to be the highest proportion of any country in the Empire.

The losses have also been high - 1,165 have been killed serving with the British and Colonial forces. As many again have been wounded or taken prisoner. 260 decorations for gallantry have been awarded to our men, including two Victoria Crosses.

The Steam Packet Company have lost a further two ships, making a total of four of the 12 requisitioned by the Admiralty. In June, the *Snaefell* was returning from the Dardanelles when she was sunk in the Mediterranean by a torpedo. It has also been revealed that the *Empress Queen* was lost after hitting rocks off the Isle of Wight.

The war ended with a notable triumph for the Steam Packet's vessel *King Orry*. On 21st November, the German High Fleet sailed into captivity, to be met by the British Grand Fleet based at Scapa Flow. They sailed under Sir David Beatty and it was the *King Orry* which led the scores of German warships in the great surrender. She was the sole representative of the little ships of the Mercantile Marine which had also played a gallant part in the war. The *King Orry* is expected back in Douglas next year.

"IT'S A FACT" by DUSTY

"A MANX SHIP DID LEAD THEM".

THE 'KING ORRY' WAS THE SOLE REPRESENTATIVE OF THE BRITISH MERCANTILE MARINE AT THE SURRENDER OF THE IMPERIAL GERMAN FLEET AT SCAPA FLOW. NOV. 21ST 1918.

SHE WENT SOME LITTLE DISTANCE TO SEA, MET THE INCOMING ENEMY FLEET, AND LED THEM TO THE BRITISH FLEET WHICH LAY WAITING. 'KING ORRY' WAS THEN GIVEN PRIDE OF PLACE IN THE CENTRE OF THE LINE, BY ADMIRAL BEATTY.

WITH ACKNOWLEDGEMENTS TO 'BURGESS', AND THE I.O.M. SPECULATA

HUMAN HAIR JEWELLERY.

STRANGE TASTE IN JEWELLERY WAS IN VOGUE ON THE ISLAND. SOME YEARS AGO, WHEN MANX PEOPLE WORE EAR-RINGS, BROOCHES, NECKLACES, ETC., MADE OF THE HAIR OF RELATIVES, FRIENDS AND EVEN THEIR OWN HAIR.

THE DESIGNS & CRAFTSMENSHIP WERE EXCEEDINGLY FINE.

CANINE FOOTBALLER.

'BOB', ROUGH-HAIRED TERRIER, BELONGING TO MR. HUGHES, MANAGER OF A DOUGLAS CINEMA, PLAYS FOOTBALL WITH A TENNIS BALL. WEARING SPECIALLY MADE FOOTBALL BOOTS, HE HAS APPEARED IN PATHIETONE FILMS, IN THIS ROLE.

"IT'S A FACT" by DUSTY.

"A Link with Bligh of the Bounty"

RIFLED!

"BAD OLD DAYS"

A FAST CRUMBLING LINK WITH ADMIRAL BLIGH, COMMANDER OF THE BOUNTY, (THE MUTINY ON WHICH, WAS SO PECULIARLY MANX,) LIES IN ONCHAN CHURCHYARD, IT IS THE TOMB OF MARY & RICHARD BETHAM, MOTHER & FATHER OF THE GIRL WHOM BLIGH MARRIED IN ONCHAN CHURCH.

THE DATES ON THE GRAVE ARE 1766 MARY & 1789 RICHARD. THE STONE IS STILL GOOD, BUT SHABBY THROUGH NEGLECT.

A WHIPPING POST FOR WOMEN STILL STANDS IN ONCHAN, AND THO' IT IS NOW, BUT PART OF THE CHURCHYARD WALL SOME MEN HAVE BEEN KNOWN TO CAST AFFECTIONATE GLANCES AT IT.

IN 1864 THE ADMIRALTY WERE AMAZED TO DISCOVER THAT THE I.O.M. POSSESSED 6 MUZZLE LOADING CANNON THAT WERE RIFLED, THEY DATE FROM THE 16TH CENTURY, LONG BEFORE THE DAYS OF SHELLS, THE ROYAL ARTILLERY INSTITUTE, WOOLWICH, WERE SO INTRIGUED, THAT THEY RETAINED 4 OF THEM AS THE WORLD'S EARLIEST KNOWN EXAMPLES OF RIFLING. THE OTHER TWO NOW ADORN OUR MUSEUM.

IT'S A FACT by DUSTY.

GREAT EXPECTATIONS!

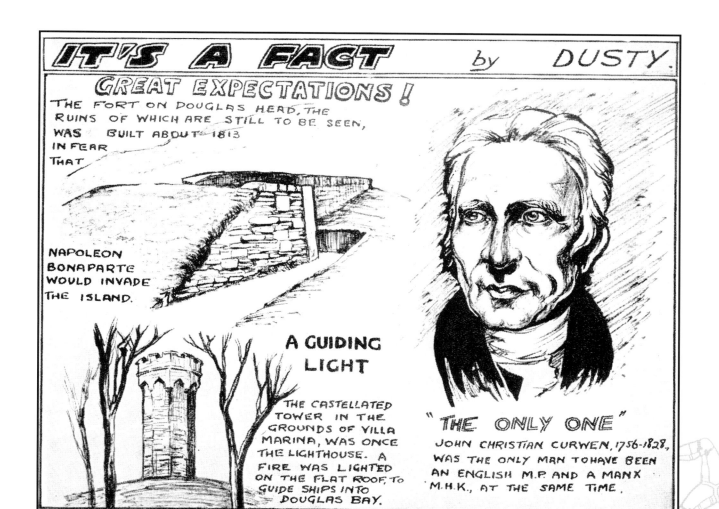

THE FORT ON DOUGLAS HEAD, THE RUINS OF WHICH ARE STILL TO BE SEEN, WAS BUILT ABOUT 1813 IN FEAR THAT NAPOLEON BONAPARTE WOULD INVADE THE ISLAND.

A GUIDING LIGHT

THE CASTELLATED TOWER IN THE GROUNDS OF VILLA MARINA, WAS ONCE THE LIGHTHOUSE. A FIRE WAS LIGHTED ON THE FLAT ROOF, TO GUIDE SHIPS INTO DOUGLAS BAY.

"THE ONLY ONE"

JOHN CHRISTIAN CURWEN, 1756-1828, WAS THE ONLY MAN TO HAVE BEEN AN ENGLISH M.P. AND A MANX M.H.K., AT THE SAME TIME.